Behind Church Doors:

Overcoming Church Hurt

Second Edition

Alaina Holloway-Carpenter

Copyright © 2018 Alaina Holloway-Carpenter

All rights reserved. No part of this publication may be reproduced, distributed, or transmitted in any form or by any means, including photocopying, recording, or other electronic or mechanical methods, without the prior written permission of the publisher, except in the case of brief quotations embodied in critical reviews and certain other noncommercial uses permitted by copyright law. For permission requests, write to the author, addressed "Attention: Permissions," at the email address below.

alainacarpenter@yahoo.com

Printed in the United States of America

ISBN: 978-0-9998274-6-8 (Paperback)

Dedication

I am dedicating this book to my daughters, Lauren Ashley and Allyson Nicole. You are the reasons that I never gave up! You have endured some harsh realities, yet you have been able to remain resilient. What you both have endured as children most adults could not handle. Use this as a stepping-stone into your destinies, not making any excuses for delay. My prayer is that you will continue to keep God first in everything that you do. Thank you for believing in me and pushing me. We have and always will be a *team*. I love you, and continue to soar. The sky is the limit.

Disclaimer

This is a memoir. The events are portrayed to the best of Alaina Holloway-Carpenter's memory. While all the stories in this book are true, some names and identifying details have been changed to protect the privacy of the people involved.

Introduction

Church is a place where believers are supposed to assemble to praise and worship our God. From the pressures of life to the disappointments of the week, the church is where we receive our healing, deliverance, direction, and peace. Not only do we worship, but we also fellowship with our brothers and sisters in what should be a loving, nurturing, and caring atmosphere. It is a *haven of rest* from the cares of this life. When we leave this place, we should be uplifted and encouraged to continue the race.

Sadly, a significant part of my experience has been quite the opposite. The danger of moving prematurely from under our covering made us a target for Satan to do what he does best: steal, kill, and destroy.

"What sorrow awaits the leader of my people the shepherds of my sheep--for they have destroyed and scattered the very ones they were expected to care for, says the Lord" (Jer. 23:1 NLT). Unfortunately, this scripture holds true for us even today. We as Christians have made our pastors *gods*. They are supposed to protect us, the *sheep*. Instead, we have become scattered. We have covered them and kept quiet at our own expense and, in many instances, to our own detriment. We come to church masked, and afraid to uncover. We've become brainwashed and zapped of the abundant life we were destined to live.

Journey with me through the valley of the shadow of death, as this book depicts the betrayal, hurt, and humiliation that my family suffered at the hands of God's anointed. This is a story of survival through the trenches of the church world. In spite of everything we have gone through, God is still faithful to his Word concerning my family and me. He said that He would never leave us nor forsake us, and He has not failed at that yet. This story is thought provoking and it's intensity will bring about laughter, tears, frustration, and even repentance. Be blessed, encouraged, and strengthened by my transparency.

Foreword

In Genesis 22, the story is told of God telling Abraham to sacrifice his promised child as a sign of faith. This narrative is applauded and celebrated as the sign that Abraham truly had trust in God to provide. Sermons, Bible studies, commentaries, theological expositions, and devotionals have all provided tremendous insight into the lengths to which Abraham was willing to go to demonstrate his undying commitment to Yahweh. But when we look closer at the story, the person whose faith was challenged the most was not Abraham, but Isaac. Isaac was the one who was about to be murdered for the sake of Abraham's relationship with God.

Everyone celebrates Abraham, but no one discusses Isaac. Abraham receives the title of "father of the faith" while Isaac bears the burden of faith-based trauma. In essence, Isaac becomes a victim of "church hurt." Isaac was put on the altar of Abraham's ministry ambitions. While he was never stabbed by his father's dagger, he cannot un-see the sharp point of its blade glistening in the Mesopotamian sun. Isaac cannot un-feel the rope's rough edges tightly gripping his skin. Those memories haunted Isaac every time he overheard his father mention that he had a conversation with God. The traumatic experiences stalked him as he moved into adulthood. It affected the way that he raised his children, and ultimately stunted his growth as a man of God. He became the least accomplished of the Hebrew patriarchs.

Just like Isaac, so many of God's children have become victims of "church hurt" at the hands of those considered heroes in the faith. Great women and men of God often place the lives of their sisters and brothers in Christ on the altars of "kingdom advancement." And people will celebrate them as people of faith without acknowledging the people that were either unknowingly or intentionally traumatized by the church. In the aftermath of the reality of this trauma, we are left to ask the question: Who ministers to Isaac after Abraham threatens to kill him?

I believe that *Behind Church Doors: Overcoming Church Hurt* attempts to answer that question for every believer who has been scarred and bruised by the Church. Alaina Holloway-Carpenter, a modern-day Isaac, tells the story of her resilience in the midst of church hurt in a way that allows the reader to see how God can heal our deepest wounds. Her testimony is one that follows the Isaiah 61 proclamation that God has "given her the garment of praise for the spirit of heaviness!" Reading this book will cause you to deal with the deepest and darkest pains that you have been trying to avoid, all while illustrating the emotional and spiritual healing of Jesus Christ.

I pray that as you turn these pages, God will open up your heart and your mind to receive comfort conviction, honesty and healing, and that Alaina's story will meet you in the place where you need the touch of God the most. You do not have to let church hurt destroy you, your family, or your future! You can be resilient! May this book bless you as much as Alaina has blessed me!

Melech E. M. Thomas

November 2015

Contents

Introduction v

Foreword vii

Contents ix

Chapter 1: Uninvited Guest 1

Chapter 2: Why Her? 20

Chapter 3: My Wedding Night 28

Chapter 4: Out of My Character 36

Chapter 5: Just Stand 52

Chapter 6: Lights, Camera, Action 74

Chapter 7: Talk of the Town 91

Chapter 8: The Counseling Session 95

Chapter 9: No Payment 106

Chapter 10: The Job Offer 108

Chapter 11: Atlanta–A New Beginning 112

Chapter 12: A Whirlwind 115

Chapter 13: My Unforgettable Encounter 119

Chapter 14: Hurt People Hurt People 123

Chapter 15: Motives 146

Chapter 16: Moving Day 150

Chapter 17: The Friendship 152

Chapter 18: The Salon 154

Chapter 19: True Colors 161

Chapter 20: Walking Away 170

~~The Conclusion~~ - The Beginning 174

Church Should be a Hospital 178

The Altar Call 183

CHAPTER 1

Uninvited Guest

It was April 26, 2005, and I was so excited because it was my baby girl's birthday. Allyson was turning nine years old and birthdays were a big deal in our family. I got up, ran into her room, hopped on her bed, and began singing "Happy birthday to you, happy birthday to you, happy birthday to Allyson, happy birthday to you!" She was happy to be turning the big nine. This was really important to Allyson because she was always the youngest in her class, and at the age of nine, she was already in the fifth grade.

I said, "Allyson, get up and go get ready for school."

As she headed to the bathroom, I went and got one of her gifts and set it on her bed. It was what she would wear to school. As she came back to her room, she saw a big Gap bag, and she knew it was for her.

She tore open the bag, and said, "Mommy, I love it."

It was a funny shade of green jogging suit with the cream Gap logo on the sweatshirt.

I smiled, and said, "Get dressed."

Her big sister, Lauren, came in the room to say happy birthday. Both of the girls got dressed and then came upstairs to get their hair done. As I did Allyson's hair, I explained to her that because today was Tuesday, we would celebrate her birthday on the upcoming Saturday with the rest of the family, but I had gotten cupcakes for her class.

She said, "Ok."

I looked her over, and she was cute as a button.

Allyson asked, "Mommy, do I have to wear these pink and green bows in my hair? I have on a jogging suit."

I said, "Yes, Allyson, it makes the outfit."

She absolutely hated bows. As we prepared to leave, I told the girls to grab their jackets because it was a little chilly outside.

I asked the girls, "Do you have your lunches?"

"Yes, ma'am," they both answered.

"Do you have your homework?"

"Yes, ma'am," they both answered again.

"Do you have your book bags?"

"Yes, ma'am," they said.

It was very important that I asked these questions daily because we did not live in the same school district that the girls attended any longer. We were about twenty-five minutes away, so if they forgot something, we were in trouble. This was very frustrating for us because we used to live across the street from Allyson's school and ten minutes from Lauren's school, but Al wanted to leave the home that we had purchased three years prior so that he could be closer to *The Church*. Every day, I would take Lauren to Roxboro Middle School and Allyson to Boulevard Elementary School. Today was no different. I dropped Lauren off and then Allyson. I walked in her school with her cupcakes, and we went to her class. I kissed her and headed to work. I was running a little behind.

BEHIND CHURCH DOORS

At this time, I was managing a J. C. Penney's salon at Richmond Mall. Although I was happy about Allyson's birthday, I was feeling very heavy on the inside. I was angry with Al for forcing us to leave the beautiful home in Cleveland Heights that we had worked so hard to purchase. He wanted to move to a home in Maple Heights to be close to a church that the girls and I did not want to be at. We went from homeowners to renters. It was not an upgrade, but it was a downsize in every way.

We previously lived on historic Euclid Heights Boulevard, and our home was absolutely beautiful. It had five bedrooms, one and a half baths, and a living room with a fireplace. There were French doors connecting to our formal dining room, and a small room that was off our newly remodeled kitchen. I called this my quiet room. It was where I would go and pray or just sit and read. The house had hardwood floors throughout and a fully finished basement. It was over twenty-four hundred square feet with a huge front porch, large white pillars, a double deck, and a two-and-a-half car garage. We loved this house! So for us to walk away from it, to move to a nine-hundred-square-foot matchbox, had been mindboggling.

I arrived to work thirty minutes late and as I parked my car I felt numb. I was lethargic. It was as if something just was not right. I went on with my day, and several people asked me if I was ok. I responded, "I'm ok, but I'm just a little tired." By this time, I had learned to cover up everything. On my lunch break, I went into the mall to continue picking up things for Allyson's birthday. Shopping normally made me feel better, but not this time. As I continued to walk around the mall, I began to think *"God, what is going on? I feel like something is not right."* I just could not put my finger on it.

As I went back to work, I could not shake this feeling. It was as if I were getting sick to my stomach. The last time I felt like this was when I dreamt that something bad was going to happen to someone in my family. *"Lord, is someone about to die?"* I asked. I was preparing myself for the worst.

Back when I had this dream, it felt so real. It felt as if God was warning me. In that dream, the Lord showed me everything in this house, including the burnt wallpaper and the appliances in the kitchen that were all in the middle of the floor. The stairs leading up had large burnt holes in them. I called my grandfather on my dad's side, because I thought the dream was about him and that he was about to die. He had been sick for a while. I prayed with him and had him call family members to get things right so that his transition would be smooth. My grandfather was a mess, and he had to get some things in order. In the dream, there were two people who died. I could not figure out who the second person was. It was the most frightening thing that had ever happened to me. I could not breathe because it was so detailed.

That dream literally took my breath away. This was the same feeling that I was having all that day. *"Lord, is someone about to die?"* I asked myself again. I was preparing myself for the worst because I had that dream on a Sunday night and woke up on that Monday morning hysterical. Al was scared to death. He woke me up from screaming, and he began praying and rebuking the devil. He thought I was having a nightmare.

"This is not the devil. This is a warning from God," I told Al. I explained to him in detail about the dream. It was very strange to Al. We were heading to a hospital or somewhere to receive bad news, but we were not driving. Vee was driving like a maniac, and Bishop's wife was in the passenger seat with this big black hat and a long black coat. I explained to Al that we were in the backseat and Lauren was in the middle standing up. When we arrived at our destination, there was people were everywhere. I saw police cars with bright lights, and Bishop was there consoling my mom.

Al had a perplexed look on his face. He had heard about me and my dreams from family members. I called my mother to tell her what I had dreamt. She said, "Oh Lord!" She knew firsthand that if I dreamt it, it was coming to pass. It was a gift that I had since I was a child. I then called Bishop, who was my pastor, to tell him and his wife what had happened and that they were in my dream. The next Friday night, I received a frantic call from my mother, screaming that my grandfather and first cousin on her side were trapped in the house, and it was on fire.

"Alaina, your dream you had," she yelled.

In tears, I asked, "Mommy, are they ok?"

"I don't know! Help me, Jesus!" she was screaming at the top of her lungs.

"I'm on my way, Mommy!"

Al had not made it home from work yet, so I called Bishop.

Bishop answered the phone, and said, "Praise the Lord!"

I was screaming and crying. I was talking a mile a minute, and he understood every word that I said.

He said, "Don't you drive like that. I'm sending my wife and Vee to get you. What is your grandfather's address?" Vee was the Bishop's wife's cousin, who was living with them.

"Lockyear off 79th and Superior," I replied.

"I will meet you there," he said.

Al pulled into the driveway and heard all the commotion.

He ran in and asked, "What's wrong?"

"My grandfather's house is on fire!" I yelled.

Al said, "Get Lauren ready and let's go. Vee and Bishop's wife are on their way to pick us up."

A few seconds later Vee whipped in the driveway and blew the horn. We ran out and got in the back seat.

Every detail of the dream had come true, from Vee driving us there to Bishop's wife in the passenger's seat with that big black hat and long black coat on. Al and I were in the backseat with Lauren.

Al said, "Oh my God!!!, Alaina your dream ... look at the hat...the coat..., Vee is driving, we are in the back seat...... -

The car got silent no one said a word. Vee had to be driving at least sixty miles per hour on city streets. When we arrived, all we could see were the bright lights from the fire trucks and the police. TV cameras were everywhere, and the first face I saw was Bishop's face. He was consoling my mom.

The next day as my siblings, Al, and I walked into the burned house, it was just like the dream. The appliances were in the middle of the floor where the firefighters had moved them. The wallpaper was all burned up, there were burnt holes in the stairs, and there was so much more detail. It was that same feeling that I'd felt.

As I went back to work, I couldn't shake this feeling, so I called Al, but he didn't answer. This was a little strange because he always answered my calls. I decided to leave work early, and as I was leaving, Al called me back.

I answered, and said, "Hello."

He asked, "What's up?"

"What do you mean what's up? You left this morning without saying anything. Did you even wish Allyson a happy birthday?"

"Yeah, I was just rushing, and I didn't want wake you up. Now you know I would not leave without wishing my baby a happy birthday. I will see you guys when you get home. I'm leaving work early today," he said before we ended the call.

I thought this was rather strange because you could not pay him to leave work early. *Something is not right*, I thought. I went to pick up my girls from school. I asked Allyson what she wanted for dinner. Since it was her day, she could choose. She said she wanted pizza. That was perfect because I was not in the mood to cook. I ordered pizza and wings from her favorite place called "Teresa's Pizza".

Allyson said, "Mommy, I got in trouble in class today."

"Why?" I asked. "You got in trouble on your birthday?"

"I forgot my homework."

"Allyson, didn't I ask you if you had everything this morning?"

She said, "Yes, ma'am, but I left my folder in daddy's truck."

"As soon as we get home, get the folder and put it in your book bag."

"Ok," she replied.

When we pulled up, Al had not gotten home yet, and by this time my family began to call to wish Allyson a happy birthday. As we were walking in the house, Allyson was on the phone. Al pulled up. He came into the house and began to play with the girls. Then he bypassed the pizza and the wings and went upstairs. I followed him upstairs to our bedroom.

I asked him, "Is everything ok?"

"Yes, why did you ask me that?"

I replied, "Well, it's Allyson's birthday. We were about to eat, and you're up here in the bed."

Al had been very depressed because a few weeks prior he had been demoted from executive pastor, which he had served as for three and a half years, to director of the sports ministry. He was devastated. Then he'd been asked by Pastor Herman to train his successor, which was Lady Herman's cousin. It was like something out of the movies. Al had worked so hard for this man and *The Church*. He had almost sold his soul to this man even at the expense of his family. This had been the first time that Al had made this kind of money. Although I had always made more money than Al, it had never been a problem because we were a team. We had one bank account, and we'd never talked about who made more. It hadn't been until we got to this church that the pastor had always reminded Al how much he'd been paying him. For Al, as a man, he had been excited about the money he'd been bringing home because now I hadn't had to work as hard. It made him feel better about himself. Now, I had not been at all surprised by Pastor Herman's decision. I had called it out a long time ago. He had only been using Al to get where he had wanted to be, and then I felt he would get rid of him. This had made Al not quite himself.

I remembered that Allyson had forgotten her folder in the truck. I decided to get it so she wouldn't forget it again. I went to the truck, opened the front driver's side door, and began looking for it, but I didn't see it. I couldn't help but notice the funny smell in the car, but I continued to look for the folder. I looked in the backseat and saw the folder. Instead of reaching to grab it, I walked around and opened the back passenger's side door. I noticed a six-pack of beer under the passenger's seat with only two unopened bottles. My heart fell out of my chest. *"What in the world is going on?"* I asked myself. I was filled with so much emotion and anger. *"Is this what I was feeling earlier?"* I thought. I ran into the house, and up the stairs I went.

"Al, what the hell is going on?" I asked as I shut the door, and then I threw the four empty beer bottles on the bed.

I was terrified because Al had been clean from drugs for a little over fifteen years, and I knew that alcohol could trigger his appetite for drugs. All kinds of thoughts were going through my head. *"Maybe it's not his. Please, God, no. Maybe he was counseling someone, and it's his or hers. Please let it be anybody's but his!"*

"Al, say something!" I yelled.

Finally, he opened his mouth, and said, "It's mine, Alaina. I was feeling so down about everything that had happened and how Pastor Herman had played me. I brought you and the girls to this church against your will. I should have listened to you from the beginning." "Now he gets an epiphany", I thought.

He began to explain how he had compromised and closed his eyes to so much that he didn't even know who he was anymore.

"Al, I'm not sure what all you're talking about, but what I do know is that drinking is not the answer. I'm happy that you finally see we should never have come here. We will figure it out."

"Hey, bae, I'm so sorry," he said.

Although I heard him, I felt like he was leaving something out. As I lay in the bed next to him with my head on his chest, I had to hold my breath because he reeked of alcohol.

"Al, are you sure that's all? I have had this feeling all day that something is not right," I said.

Al began to get nervous, because after being married for almost sixteen years, he knew me well enough to know that if I had those feelings I would be dead on point. He knew that that was how God would speak to me. Then out of nowhere and with no warning to him or me, it came out.

"Are you having an affair?" I asked him.

"What? Why would you ask me that?" he asked.

I had never had this feeling before.

"No," he said and then held me in his arms.

It was around 5:30 p.m. when we feel asleep. I woke up to someone knocking on the door. I looked at the clock, and it was 7:16 p.m.

I nudged Al and asked, "Are you expecting anyone?"

He grunted and appeared to be asleep. I was not expecting anyone, no one even knew our new address.

Allyson yelled, "Mommy, it's the Hermans at the door."

"The Hermans?" I asked.

"Yes, ma'am," she replied.

I thought, *"Now what do they want?"*

"Allyson, did you open the door?" I asked.

"No, ma'am," she said.

I got up and fixed myself up.

"Just a minute," I yelled.

I ran down the stairs, opened the door, and it was the Hermans.

I'm sure by the look on my face they could tell I was quite surprised.

"So what brings you all over here tonight"? I asked. "With no calls or anything."

"Well, we wanted to talk to you and Al," Pastor Herman replied.

"Ok, come in and have a seat."

I told Lauren and Allyson to go upstairs, and then I called for Al to come down. As we waited for Al, Pastor Herman began to make small talk.

He asked, "How was your day, and how are the kids?"

"Well, since you asked, it was ok, and we're celebrating Allyson's birthday today," I told him.

"Oh, I didn't know," he said.

I was so confused. He was not at all concerned about how my day went or how my kids were doing.

I wondered, *"Why are they at my house?"* They had never been over before. His wife had been over, but not him. Not only did that strike me as odd, but it was also the fact that we were not cool like that at all. Finally, I heard Al coming down the stairs. When I saw his face, I quickly realized that I was the only one that did not know why they were there. It was very apparent that they'd had a conversation without me being present.

We all were sitting down. Al and Pastor Herman were on one couch, and his wife and I were on the other. Al and I were facing each other, and Pastor Herman and his wife were facing each other. It was quiet as a church mouse, and everyone was looking suspicious except me. They were very nervous. Al never looked up. He kept his head down. The expression on Lady Herman's face was as if she was scared to death, so I knew that the feeling that I had all day was about to be revealed. In the back of my mind, I was still trying to understand why they were at my house. They did not like me at all. I was not one that Pastor Herman could control, so he tolerated me so he could continue to use Al.

After all the small talk, Pastor Herman asked, "Well, Al, do you have something you want to say?"

Now I was pissed off, because since when did we need a mediator? If we did need a mediator, it sure as hell would not have been them. Al was my best friend. We had been together off and on since I was sixteen years old. We talked about everything. *"Why would he want to talk to me in front of them?"* I asked myself. He knew better than anyone that they didn't like me, especially given how they had just played him. Really? All this was playing in my head with my stomach in knots. We continued to sit in silence with all eyes on Al. We were waiting for this big announcement while he sat there looking like he was medicated. Well, now I guess he was. After several minutes that seemed like an hour had passed, he uttered a few words.

"Well, um ... um ... um," he said.

It was so tense in the room.

I yelled, "Will you please get it out!"

All eyes were still on Al. Lady Herman was holding her hands to her chest and slightly on her neck. I knew this was not going to be pretty.

I braced myself, and then he said, "I have been having an affair with Tiffany. It was only three times, and she might be pregnant."

The room was in complete silence, and now all eyes were on me. Everyone was waiting for my response. The staring match started again. Pastor Herman looked at me, and I looked back at him. His wife also looked at me, and I looked back at her. Al never looked up. His head was still down. We sat in silence for at least three to four minutes. We were looking back and forth at each other. I was processing what had just been said. I was still wondering, *Why are they here?* I sat there poised and polished after hearing the most devastating news of my life. Lady Herman was looking extra hard at Pastor Herman and trying to insinuate that he needed to say something. Pastor Herman put his hands together and begin to rub them as he scooted to the edge of the couch.

"Sister Carpenter, did you hear what Al said?" he asked.

I just looked at him as if to say, *I know you are not talking to me.*

He called my name again, "Sister Carpenter?"

I was still looking at Al, who was still holding his head down.

"Are you going to say something?" Pastor Herman asked. "Did you hear him?"

I looked at him with sarcasm, and eventually, I nodded my head to say yes. Back to silence we went. No one knew what to do or to say, but they were waiting for a response from me, and I had none. I was still trying to figure out why he would want to talk to me in front of them. I finally thought, *Let me say something.*

I sat up, and asked Pastor Herman, "Would you please take your wife and leave my house?"

Well, I guess that was not the response that they were expecting, because his wife gasped for air.

Pastor Herman asked me again, "Did you hear what Al just said?"

I scooted to the edge of the couch like him, and then I put my hands together.

Then I asked him, "Did you hear what I said? Take your wife and get out of my house!"

"Now, Sister Carpenter, Lady Herman and I are here to support you. I know this has to be hard, but we're here," Pastor Herman stated.

I burst out in a hearty laugh and then said, "Now you're here? Really? I have been trying to talk to you for months. This is partially your fault. You have ignored me from the beginning. You have driven a wedge in this house with your unreasonable leadership and dictatorship. So now you think that I am going to sit here and become vulnerable in front of you and your wife who doesn't give a damn about me. Well, you thought wrong. Get the fuck out of my house!"

Pastor Herman sat up, and said, "I know you're hurting, and, yes, maybe we were not here for you in the past, but we're here now."

"It's too damn late. Now I'm telling you for the last time to get the fuck out of my house!"

I don't know what happened after that. I had three glass figurines on my coffee table. My head had to have spun around three times, and every piece of emotion that had built up in me came out. I jumped up and grabbed the figurines. I hit Al on the head and began to charge at him for still not saying a word. Lady Herman tried to grab me while still holding on to her fifteen-hundred-dollar Fendi bag that her husband had just bragged about buying her in the pulpit the Sunday before. I grabbed the bag and ripped it in half. I was enraged, but I didn't want to hurt her. She was pregnant and had already had two miscarriages. I knew how badly she wanted this baby.

I went into a rage and asked, "Is this the response you wanted? Now get the fuck out of here."

I was still hysterical.

Then Pastor Herman had the nerve to ask Al, "Are you ok? Do you want us to take you someplace tonight?"

Al began to mumble, "Naw--"

I interrupted, and said, "He's staying right here! He isn't going anywhere!"

In my mind, I couldn't understand why Pastor Herman would ask him that. *Why would he be trying to protect Al?*

Pastor Herman said, "Laina, I just don't want to leave and something happens. You're not in your right mind." "You damn right I'm not in my right mind it would behoove you leave NOW" I said.

In that moment, I thought of my girls upstairs. I was unsure if they could hear me. I didn't want to alarm them so I began to calm down. I was trying to hold back the tears because I didn't want to show any emotion in front of them but I couldn't hold it any longer and I broke down and began to cry. Lady Herman reluctantly tried to console me; she didn't know how I would react to what had just happened, so she quietly asked if she could talk to me in the other room for a minute. I agreed because I didn't know what else to do. We walked into Lauren's room. We both sat on the bed, and Lady Herman began to speak.

"I know this is really hard for you, and we're going to be here with you through this whole process," she stated.

Although her mouth was moving, I couldn't hear anything she was saying. I zoned out in a blank stare as if she was on mute. It seemed so fake to me, she was not a fan at all. I felt like she felt she finally had something on me.

I interrupted her and yelled, "Stop, just stop! You're saying all the right things today, but the truth of the matter is that I don't trust you or your husband. You do not nor have you ever had my best interests at heart." I don't even know why I am talking to you.

She didn't know what to say at this point. I don't think that anyone had ever been this honest with her, and I didn't have anything else to lose. I sat on my daughter's bed and began to explain how she and her husband had mistreated my family and me.

I remembered about two years prior to this day how I had shared with Al that I hated his schedule. He had been on call seven days a week, twenty-four hours a day. He had two cell phones and a pager. He had overseen most aspects of the church. This included the training of the ministers, deacons, teaching new member's class, giving premarital counseling, handling the drug ministry, security, and so much more. This had caused him to be away from our home a lot. Even when he was home, he wasn't present. Day and night he would constantly be on the phone, or responding to the pager and every call from Pastor Herman. He'd begun to miss all of our children's extracurricular activities, parent-teacher conferences, open houses, and homework time. When he did come to an event, he would be on the phone the whole time. Once I told him I couldn't even make love to him without the phone going off. This had not been how our family was used to operating. He used to pray with our girls every morning and every night. Now he was praying over them while they slept. He was getting home so late at night. We had always made time to be present for our children and for each other. I essentially had become a single parent while married.

The following Wednesday after Al and I had this conversation about his schedule, and Bible study had ended, Pastor Herman had called me to the front. He called me by beckoning me with his two fingers and not properly addressing me by name. I had looked around like *I know he is not talking to me and beckoning me as if I'm some chick off the street*. So I'd ignored him and continued to do what I had been doing. He was so ghetto no tack at all.

Finally, he'd addressed me and said, "Sister Carpenter."

I had acknowledged him and answered, "Yes."

He'd said, "Come here."

He'd begun to explain how Pastor Al had told him I had been sweating him about his hours at the church.

He'd said, "I need you to understand that we're building something right now, and it's going to take some extra time. I need you to release him and stop pressing him. In a few days, we're going to be able to live where we want to live, dress like we want to dress, and drive what we want to drive, but it's gonna take some sacrifice."

I'd stood there looking at him as if he was some character because I'd already owned my own home. We had always been together, from head to toe, and we had driven what I wanted to drive. We were not rich, but we had been content. I wouldn't respond, but I just looked at him.

After he'd seen that I had not been moved by his prosperity speech, he said, "You need to be happy that he's putting time in here, because he could be back in the crack house."

I was flabbergasted. I'd looked at him as if he was crazy, and I walked away. I thought, *like many leaders, he is taking what you share in private to blast you in public.* Al being on drugs in the past had been part of his testimony that he had not been ashamed of, but for Pastor Herman to throw it back in my face, spoke volumes about who he was as a person. In that moment, I knew Al was gone. We had never shared our personal information outside of our marital covenant. I couldn't believe that Pastor Herman was talking to me in such a derogatory manner and using ghetto street lingo.

I told Lady Herman that I would not want my worst enemy to go through what I had gone through in this ministry. This was the worst three and a half years of my life. I went on to tell her that not only was Al's schedule a problem, but also I explained how I would cry every Sunday before coming to church, trying to figure out what to wear. I had to deal with the insecurity of her and her armor-bearers who thought I was trying to be the first lady, and trying to "out dress her" when I had been dressing like this all my life. I had to let her know that not only did I not want her position, but also that I didn't even want to be at this church. I told her that we were fine where we were before coming here, and how I served her and that ministry in spite of how she treated me.

Lady Herman said, "I know you went through a lot here. I'm sorry, but we are going to do better."

I said, "I sure hope so because I'm not the only one who feels this way. I'm just the only one who is brave enough to tell you. Let's be real, because this is not our first time having this conversation. This is why I don't trust you nor am I willing to have a conversation with you about anything pertaining to my family and me. You are sitting here like you have never heard this before. This is so fake. I have been dogged out every week because of how I keep my children and myself. Lady Herman, in all the time I have been here, you can't say that I have done anything to you in a negative manner. I have supported you, and I have taken your vision of the women's ministry and gave it life. I have taught the women here how to honor and respect your position as the 'first lady' even when you didn't know what to do with your position. I fought for you even when your own husband didn't have faith that you could get the job done. I never took credit for anything I did in this church, I always explained that it was from the 'first lady' even when they knew you had nothing to do with it. I even took your daughter to New York with Lauren and me to celebrate their thirteenth birthdays. According to you, it was her first time going out of town. I did all of this and so much more, not for your approval but because it was the right and mature thing to do. I did it knowing that you didn't like me at all. Your insecurity is hurting several women in this church. You are not poor anymore. Go shopping, fix yourself up, and do your hair. Wear the appropriate size clothes. For you to treat me like you have is so "junior high-ish". Anything I do in this church is a problem. You ask me to pray at events so I do, and now I'm trying to out pray you. You and your husband put me over the women's conference; it's a success, so now I'm trying to outdo you there. You both are always talking about people being jealous of you when, in fact, you are the ones who have the problem. I have watched you dog out your childhood friends who were there for you when you had nothing; now they are jealous of you too. Those are your demons in your head lying to you. Along with your crazy-ass armor-bearers who like to feed you this nonsense. They are just as insecure as you are." Lady Herman everyone knows that your husband don't value your opinion nor does he trust you in this ministry so instead of dealing with him you try to take it out on others, it's not right.

As I reflected on what I was saying to her, it reminded me of other first ladies and their families whom I had encountered in the past. Every time I walked in a room, I could tell I was the topic of discussion. I had never done anything to her…except exist… and that was something that I could not change. I stopped a long time ago trying to figure out why she had a problem with me. It was her problem and her problem alone.

"So now you want to sit here like you have compassion and sympathy for me. All the while you are probably rejoicing, thinking that you got one up on me. You need to be worried about your own husband. Being in ministry is not new to me. I have been in leadership roles since I was thirteen years old, even on a national level. I have been mentored and taught by the best so I know how to conduct myself."

That's why I never showed publicly the way I felt about how I was being treated. No one knows, not even my closest friends. I always had your back even when you didn't have mines.

I was not quite sure if she was angry or embarrassed.

She had a bewildered look and replied, "I understand."

After speaking with her for around thirty minutes or so, I had enough, and it was time for them to leave.

I said, "I am tired, and I need some time alone."

As I walked them to the door, I looked at Al and just shook my head. I walked into Lauren's room, got in the bed, and cried myself to sleep. I was up and down all night through silent cries.

CHAPTER 2

Why Her?

It was Wednesday morning, and although I had received the worst news of my life, I still had to go on with the routine of being a mother. I got up and I fixed breakfast, I got the girls up and did their hair. I was then asked 101 questions by Allyson.

"Mommy, why did we sleep in your bed last night? Why is Daddy in my bed? Where did you sleep? What's wrong with your eyes?" she rattled off several questions at one time.

I answered what I could, and then I said, "Allyson, just be quiet and get ready for school."

Lauren quietly watched me.

Now Al was given time off from *The Church* until they could decide what to do with him. I went into Allyson's room, which was where he was sleeping. I told him that we would talk when I got back. I called JCPenney and took the day off. I explained that I had a family emergency. After I dropped the girls off at school, I was filled with so much grief. I drove to our old house on Euclid Heights Boulevard. I pulled to the backyard, turned the car off, and just lost it. I cried hard as I asked, "*Why, God, why?*" It hurt so badly. I had never felt pain like that before. I was doubled over. I had my head in the steering wheel, and I was beating on the dashboard. "*How am I going to deal with this? What am I going to tell my kids? What is my family going to think? How will The Church be affected?"* I asked myself all these questions. And to think, Tiffany also might be pregnant! In my heart, I didn't believe that she could be pregnant. She had just had a baby a few months ago. In the midst of all my anguish and grief, I could not stop thinking, *Why Tiffany?*

Tiffany had come into our lives ten months prior. She had made an appointment to speak to a pastor at *The Church*. She'd ended up in Pastor Al's office. She was there to request financial assistance because she was in the process of being evicted. She had two daughters, ages two and four. She was also three months' pregnant. After Al had met with her, he felt that she could benefit from meeting with me. So he called me and asked if I could meet with her that day, I said yes I'm downtown. After she left his office he called me back and said that she had two beautiful girls and that he thinks that I am going to like her. Now, this had been nothing unusual, because I had regularly counseled the women of *The Church* every Monday and Wednesday. Tiffany met me for lunch downtown at Houlihan's. Al had given her bus fare for her and her children. When she approached me, I couldn't help but notice that her children were absolutely beautiful and well kept. She presented well in appearance which is not what I was expecting to see. In our conversation we talked about her life. She explained that she had been in foster care, since she was two years old, and was regularly abused by men. She began stripping at the age of thirteen and using men for money. It was a way of survival, which resulted in her being moved from home to home. She came to *The Church* because she wanted help and to begin a new life.

In the midst of all this turmoil, divorce never crossed my mind. My commitment was to Al, but my vow was to God. I took my vows very seriously. As I backed out of the driveway and headed home, I saw that I had missed several phone calls from Al, my mom, and my friend Mona.

I called Al first, and once he answered, I said, "Yes."

He was crying so hard into the phone that I could not make out what he was saying. I was only getting bits and pieces.

"I'm sorry! I'm so sorry! You didn't deserve this. Please don't leave. I don't want to lose my family," he said.

I stopped him and asked, "Where are you?"

He said, "At home."

"I'm on my way. I will talk to you then. The phone is not the place for this conversation."

Driving home, I didn't want to call my mom or my sister because they would *be able to* tell something was wrong by just hearing my voice. I was not ready to talk to them yet. I called Mona.

She asked, "Is everything ok?"

I wondered why Mona would start the conversation like that seeing that I had not told her anything. By the sound of her voice, I could tell that she knew something. *"Wow, is it already being spread?"* I asked myself. Had the Hermans called her and informed her what was going on? Anyway, this wasn't the time to figure it out. I was hurting and I needed my friend.

I said, "All hell has broken loose."

This was the first time that I had talked to anyone since I heard the news.

Mona asked, "What's wrong?"

I began to weep and said, "I'm sick to my stomach."

Mona was very hyper, pushy, and very controlling. She hated to be left in the dark about anything.

She pleaded, "What is it? Tell me because you're scaring me!"

I was too hurt and embarrassed to even begin to utter the words about what happened.

She asked, "Are you at work?"

I said, "No, I'm heading home."

She said, "I'm on my way."

I yelled, "No! I will call you later. Mona, can I ask you for a favor?"

"Yes, Alaina, what is it?"

"Will you pray for strength for me, because I need it?" I asked her.

"Yes!" she answered. "Alaina, you're scaring me! Is it your girls?"

"No," I replied.

"Is it your mother?"

"No," I said, again.

She paused and then asked, "What did Al do?"

I didn't answer, but by the outburst of crying, she knew it was him. Now, at this time, everybody loved Al. He was the coolest guy ever. He had helped so many people and was always conscience of other people's needs. Everyone knew that Al loved God, his wife, his children, and in that order. We had our issues, but we were a couple that a lot of people looked up to. Al and I were best friends.

I told Mona, "Al had an affair."

She seemed shocked and asked, "No, you are lying. With who? Wait. Are you ok? Where are the girls? How did you find out?"

Mona had a thousand questions.

I said, "I will call you back. I just made it home."

I pulled in the driveway, turned off the car, and took a deep breath. I got out and walked in the side door. Dylan, our four-week-old black shih tzu, came running to greet me. We had just gotten him two weeks prior from my friend Monique. Little did we know, he would be a source of strength for me and my girls in this process. I put Dylan in his cage and headed upstairs. As I entered the room, Al sat there on the bed, looking a mess and still holding his head down. He could not look at me at all. I wanted to be angry and fight, but I couldn't. I just looked at him.

Finally, I asked, "Al, what were you thinking? Really? How could you do this to us? How many times? Did you screw her in my bed? Where were my kids? Where were her kids? What, when, why, who? Do you love her? She was like our child. Her kids called us Nana and Papa. Hell, she called us Ma and Dad. How could you fuck your daughter? She was only twenty-four years old. Who all knew?"

I was asking so many questions that Al didn't know which one to answer first.

"You were her pastor! This is so foul!" I shouted.

Al responded reluctantly with a quiet voice, "Bishop knows."

"How in the hell does Bishop know?" I yelled.

Bishop was the pastor of the church that we left to come and join the ministry with the Herman's at *The Church*. We should have never left Bishop in the first place. Al began to explain that he could not handle what he had done. He didn't trust anybody at *The Church*, so he went back home to his father in the gospel. He went to Bishop and told him what he had done.

"What did Bishop say?" I asked.

"He said I needed to tell Pastor Herman, that he was my pastor now.

He also said that he was very disappointed in me."

"Wow," I replied. "That's all he said?"

Al also told me that Pastor Herman said he would be having a meeting with all the leaders of the church to let them know what has happened.

"Oh my God!" I yelled as I lost it again, and I started crying. "What about this baby? Do you think she is pregnant?"

Al could not handle what I was asking.

He said, "I need to go and think. I can't handle this right now."

I yelled, "You need to go think! Nigga, you have lost your damn mind!"

I never knew how selfish Al was until that moment.

"If anyone needs to think or needs time, it's me!" I yelled.

Al could not answer any of my questions.

He said, "Alaina, please, I don't want to lose my family over this."

I replied, "You selfish ass. You should've thought about that before! Get out!"

The phone rang, and it was Mona. I was still crying.

Once I answered, she asked, "I just saw Al leave, so can I come in?"

"Why are you outside my house? I told you that I would call you later."

She said, "I was concerned, and I wanted to make sure you were all right."

Mona had to know something, but I was too upset to try to figure it out. The reality was I needed a friend.

I went and opened the door to let her in. Now Mona was not affectionate at all. I mean there was not an affectionate bone in her body, but I just wanted to fall in her arms and cry. I just sat on the couch.

She walked in behind me and said, "I'm so sorry. I saw Al, but he didn't say anything."

As she sat down, I began to tell her everything that had happened the night before with the Hermans. Mona and I could always find something to laugh about, even in the most difficult times.

She asked, "You cursed at Pastor Herman?"

I said, "Yes."

"I keep telling everybody your ass is crazy," she said. "You ripped her purse in half?"

I answered, "Yep, sure did."

"Wow! I have never seen you like that. I can't even imagine."

I looked at her, and said, "Please don't say anything to anyone. I know it's going to be in the streets."

She said, "You know I won't say anything, Alaina."

I just looked at her and said, "Like I said, don't say nothing to nobody."

Mona talked a lot.

She asked, "Have you eaten anything today?"

I replied, "No, I don't have an appetite."

"Do you want me to get you something to eat?"

"No, Mona," I said. "I feel helpless."

"What can I do?"

"Can you pick up my girls from school today? I'm tired. I've been up all night and haven't had any sleep. I don't know what I'm going to do or say to them yet. This is going to kill them."

She said, "Yes, and I'll get them something to eat so you don't have to worry about cooking tonight."

As Mona was leaving, I said, "I love you."

She said, "You're going to be all right. Alaina, you're going to get through this."

Mona was eight and a half months pregnant at this time. She brought my girls home around six o'clock that evening. I still had not been to sleep or had anything to eat. I realized I had not heard from Al, so I called him and his phone went straight to voicemail. Here came that feeling again. My mind went back to that six-pack of beer that I found in the back of the truck. Had it triggered his appetite for drugs?

God, no! Please no! I can't go through this again! I thought. Al had been clean for fifteen years. The first six months of our marriage were a nightmare. My wedding night was the worst night of my life. At that moment, I felt like Job 3:25-26 which says "What I always feared has happened to me. What I dreaded has come true. *I have no peace, no quietness. I have no rest; only trouble comes.*"

CHAPTER 3

My Wedding Night

January 17, 1991, started like any regular day. I was very sad because the day before my only brother was sent off to Saudi Arabia for the war. I remember so well that it was on a Thursday. I got up to get ready for work. I was working at Hair Essence Beauty Salon. I had booked only a few clients that day so that I could be done by five o'clock. It was very cold that day. It was a low of about nine degrees. It was so grey outside. As I was taking my bath, I sat in the tub, and I was asking myself, *"Why am I going to work on my wedding day?"* My original date to get married was June 29, 1991.

My mom and I had planned a beautiful wedding. I would be her first daughter to get married. My colors were buff ivory, gold, and black with a touch of red. The wedding would start at 6:45 p.m. I always wanted an after-five wedding. We had met with several people to prepare for this fabulous wedding. We met with a seamstress, wedding coordinator, photographer, florists, and caterers. I was going to have five bridesmaids, two flower girls, a ring bearer, and six hosts and hostesses. My uncle Al would give me away. My father had died when I was fourteen years old. I had contacted gospel singer Rodney Posey to sing at my wedding. He was ecstatic because he had watched me grow up and was very proud of me. It would be the wedding I had always dreamed of. It would be simple but elegant. I would get married at an historic Pentecostal church in the City of Cleveland. It was so beautiful inside from the ceilings to the floor, and very Victorian. There was hand-painted art on the ceilings, mahogany pillars in the pulpit, and beautiful stained-glass windows. I would walk in to Rodney Posey singing "Holy," which was a hit from his first album. Michael Pickett would be on the piano, and Professor Richard Smith would be on the organ. The background singers would be friends that I had grown up with singing in the Greater Cleveland Choral Chapter. Brenda Waters would sing "The Lord's Prayer," and Hortense Crawford would sing "We Shall Behold Him." I, my new husband, and the wedding party would exit on Handel's "Messiah" arranged by Quincy Jones. It was going to be the greatest singing ever. I wanted my wedding to be one that you would not soon forget. I could not wait for the great Bishop to preach to us. At my church, he would not just perform a ceremony; you would get a Word. He would preach one of his hallmark sermons, "What To Do When Blue Skies Turn Gray." The reception would follow, and it would be at the Lander Haven Country Club. The menu would be simple but elegant. We would have a stretch limo and drive around the City of Cleveland proclaiming that we were now married. We would honeymoon in Jamaica. None of this took place because I found out that I was pregnant. We felt it was better to prepare for our baby than to pay for a wedding.

I was done with my clients at around 3:30 p.m. I counted my money, and I had made four hundred and twenty dollars that day. My friend Denise did my hair. I left the salon and went back to my apartment. When I got home, I ran water to take another bath, and my sister Dee Dee called.

She asked, "Are you scared?"

I replied, "No."

"Do you need me to drive you to the church?" she asked me.

Again, I replied, "No."

Al was going to come with his friend Ron, and we were going to drive my car back to the apartment.

She said, "Ok, I love you, and I'll see you at the church."

I sat on my bed because my brother was in the war. He had no clue that his baby sister was getting married, and that I had moved my wedding date from June to January. My heart was also heavy because one of the men I admired the most, Bishop, was not marrying me. He wouldn't even give me his blessing to marry Al. He was very disappointed. He had advised me to wait before marrying Al. He said I should wait until he was more stable and had something to bring to the table like a steady job, more clean time off drugs for at least a year, and his own place. *Oh no, I would not listen, because I was in love!*

As I continued to get dressed, my heart was so heavy, but I could not articulate why. I went to my closet and pulled out this off-white suit and pair of cream shoes. I did not like my outfit at all. This was the suit I would wear for communion on first Sundays, but not my wedding day. I got dressed and my heart was even heavier. I had to pull it off. I didn't want to be embarrassed.

I could hear Bishop's voice as he said, *"Not yet, Alaina. Wait! You don't have to get married just because you're pregnant."* Then he clapped his hands and said, *"Do as you please. You do not have my blessings."*

Then he shooed me off with his hands. I can still hear the ringing of his clap. After I did my make-up I thought *"I will show Bishop that my marriage can work."* I began to walk to my car. I was supposed to be happy, but I was so sad. I got to the church that Al was attending, which would soon be my new church home. I pulled into the parking lot and shook my head. The church had just moved to this location. It used to be a club that I had gone to a few years back. No one was there. The pastor and his wife were late, so I sat in my car. Finally, he and his wife pulled up. We went in, and I sat in the back, waiting for my mother and my sister. I looked around and gasped for air because my church home had such a beautiful sanctuary. Now I was sitting in what used to be a bar. The church had no windows. The walls on what they had made the altar and pulpit were painted black.

After a while, my family arrives, my mother, sister, godmother, and god-sister. Soon after, Al came in with his father and his friend Ron. His mother finally arrived with his cousin and her daughter. The pastor called Al and me up. Al gave me a dozen roses that he had picked up from the mall that had begun to wilt. I said thank you. He was smiling from ear to ear. The pastor's wife sang "The Lord's Prayer," and that was the extent of the singing. The pastor began to pray for us, and we began to perform the vows.

Then we got to the part where the pastor asked, "Who gives this bride to be married to this man?"

It hit me that there was no one to give me away.

Then my mom and sister at the same time said, "We do."

Everyone kind of chuckled. I thought, *What a mess.* He pronounced us man and wife, and then we kissed. We left the church after we greeted the nine people who attended. As we drove back to my apartment, I thought it would be nice to stop and get a bottle of champagne and some strawberries for us to celebrate. Even though I didn't drink, I thought every groom and bride were supposed to make a toast. We stopped at the corner store by the apartment. I gave Al a twenty-dollar bill. I had to give him the twenty because he had spent all of his money on the wilted roses. He came out of the store. They did not have champagne, so he bought a bottle of Reunite.

He got in the car, and said, "All right, let's go and consummate our wedding, Mrs. Carpenter."

As we entered my apartment, I thought I would go put on my lingerie, but we never made it to the bedroom. He took that bottle of Reunite, with his coat still on, and tried to open it.

I said, "Al, can you slow down? Get me a glass."

I wanted to feed him strawberries and make a toast. Before I knew it, he had turned the bottle upside down and pretty much downed the whole thing. I remember thinking that I wished he would slow down. He was more concerned with taking a drink than celebrating our union. He had this look in his eyes that scared me. I had never seen that look before.

I said, "Let's go into the bedroom."

He said, "No, let's consummate it right here in the living room."

It was horrible. There was no foreplay. It was painful, because I was not lubricated. He was rushing. I felt like Ms. Celie in *The Color Purple* when Mister would get on top of her and do his business. Eventually we got in the bed. I wanted to snuggle, but he went into a deep sleep, or so I thought. I woke up an hour or two later to find Al gone. I got up, looked around my apartment, and there was no Al. I went and opened the door, and I was surprised. My whole door was covered with paper that read, *Congratulations*. There was also a basket with chocolates and two mugs that had something about love and marriage written on them. I thought maybe Al did this, and he was trying to surprise me. I picked up the basket, brought it in, and went into my room. I took a shower and put on the lingerie that I had wanted to wear earlier. I went and laid down, waiting for Al to return. I had a very uneasy feeling, so I took the money I had made out of my purse and put it inside my pillowcase. I heard the door open. Al came in and sat on the bed with his coat on.

I asked, "Where have you been?"

He said, "I went to my mother's house to get the rest of my clothes."

I asked, "Oh, so where are your clothes?"

"I left them in the car. I'll bring them up in the morning."

I said, "Al, take off your coat and get in the bed."

He said, "I need a few dollars."

"What?"

He said, "I need a few dollars."

"Its two o'clock in the morning. Plus, you didn't give me the change from the store when you got the Reunite."

He jumped up and asked, "Where is your money? I know you worked today."

He grabbed my purse and started going through it.

I yelled, "Give me my purse!" We began to struggle. "What's wrong with you? Why are you acting like this? You're scaring me."

He said, "I'm outta here."

"Don't leave! Where are you going?"

I threw on a jogging suit, grabbed a jacket, and flew after him, going down three flights of stairs. My feet never touched one stair. He was acting like a crazy man. I had never seen anything like this. He jumped in his car and locked the doors so I could not get in.

As he started the car, I was banging on the windows, and yelling, "Al! Al, let's talk! Let me in! What's wrong?"

He looked at me with that look in his eyes.

He said, "Go back in the house!"

I jumped on the hood of the car to try to stop him from leaving.

I said, "If you pull off, you're going to kill me and your baby."

"If you don't get off this car I'm going to pull off," he said.

I don't know how I did this. When he rolled the down the window just a little, I took my foot and pushed the window all the way down while I was still on the hood. I climbed through the window to where I was sitting on his lap and we were face-to-face. That look in his eyes was so demonic. All I could do was call on the name of Jesus.

"Al, Al! Somebody come and help me!" I yelled, but nobody came.

He said, "I'm not playing with you, Alaina! Get off of me! I'm going to get high!"

I didn't know what to do because I was so scared. I began to do what I saw the people at my Pentecostal church do. I called on the name of Jesus.

I grabbed his mouth and told him, "Say Jesus. Just call his name, Al! If you say his name, there is deliverance. Just say his name, Al!"

I was talking into his ear and speaking to his spirit.

I said, "Say Jesus."

"Jesus!" he said in an audible voice. "If you don't get the fuck off of me, I'm going to drive with you on me!"

He began to rev the engine. When I saw that he was not playing and my deliverance session was not working, I got in the passenger's seat.

I said, "Then I'm going with you." I was hoping that it would change his mind, but it didn't. I began to pray out loud, "Father, in the name of Jesus."

He said, "Shut up! Shut the fuck up!"

All the while, he was driving like a maniac and flying down Buckeye. I was out of resources.

I began to scream, and cry, "My baby! My baby! My stomach! I'm in so much pain! I think I'm having a miscarriage!"

I should have won an Oscar that night because it worked. His mind started coming back.

He said, "Oh my God! I'm sorry! Lord, please don't let my baby die!"

I continued with the charade, acting as if I was having a miscarriage.

"Take me to the hospital right now," I yelled. All the while, I was praying, "Lord, please don't let my baby die." I was so good I convinced myself that I was really having one.

He took me to St. Luke's Hospital. I had to play this thing all the way out, so we did an ultrasound and the whole nine. They kept me there for observation for three hours. That was long enough for him to come down off of whatever he was on. *"What have I gotten myself into?"* This was supposed to be my wedding night. We were at the hospital, and he was scared to death. He would not leave my side, and he kept promising that he would never do this again. They released me around five o'clock in the morning. I did not know that drinking alcohol would trigger him to do drugs. I began to blame myself. I figured I should have never wanted champagne on my wedding night, so I forgave him. It was partially my fault, or so I thought. It was our little secret. I didn't tell a soul. But my friends Mona and Denise did see Al leave my apartment. They were the ones who had decorated my door and left the basket for me.

CHAPTER 4

Out of My Character

It was after nine o'clock and no Al. I got my kids ready for bed.

"Mommy, where is Daddy?" they asked.

He normally prayed over them every night.

I said, "He's working late tonight."

With lumps in my throat, I prayed for them. I laid down at around ten thirty. I prayed, *"Lord please don't let anything happen to him. Cover him and keep him."* At around eleven fifteen, my phone rang. *"Oh my God, is it Al?"* I asked myself.

"Hello, hello!" said the voice on the other end of the phone. "Sister Carpenter, this is Pastor Herman. Sorry for calling so late, but is Al there?"

I said, "No."

There were tears streaming down my face.

He asked, "When is the last time you heard from him?"

I answered, "This morning. Is everything okay?"

I could tell by his tone that he knew something.

He said, "I don't want to upset you, but I got a call from Tiffany. She said Al came over her house acting crazy. He locked himself in the bathroom, and she could hear the flickering of a lighter."

I said, "Oh no! He is back on crack."

I had never seen him do it, nor has he ever done it in our home. I just knew that's what it was.

He asked, "Are you sure?"

I said, "Yes."

He said, "Try to get some rest, and if you hear from him call me."

After I got off the phone with Pastor Herman, I got up, grabbed my purse, and got my wallet. I took out my debit card and looked for the customer service number on the back.

I called it and said, "Can you check, please? I believe my debit card was stolen yesterday. Can you please tell me if it had been used?"

She came back and asked, "When was the last time and where did you use it?"

I replied, "We got gas yesterday on Northfield and Libby."

She said, "Ma'am, someone has used your card nine times since yesterday and in different increments. There was one for eighty dollars, forty dollars, sixty dollars, and so on in different locations on Kinsman Avenue. They were all within an hour and a half to two hours of each other."

Before she could ask me, I asked, "Could you please put a block on that card, and how can I get my money back in my account since it was stolen and these were unauthorized purchases?"

"Right away, Mrs. Carpenter. The card has been blocked, and it will take up to forty-eight hours for the refund to reflect in your account."

I ended that call, and then I called Pastor Herman back. I told him what I had done.

He said, "Wow! I will call you back tomorrow. Please try to get some rest."

I was up all night. Every time I heard a noise or a car, I would jump. My nerves were on edge. I knew it was only a matter of time before Al would resurface because he could no longer use his debit card. I began to call Al back-to-back for two hours straight. Then I began to text him every scripture I knew, such as "Whom the son sets free is free indeed. Trust in the Lord with all your heart. There is no temptation taken you that is common to man." I texted him at least fifteen to twenty scriptures. I hoped that whenever he turned his phone back on, he would see them and that would cause him to come back home.

Al had been gone for almost three days. I sent my girls to my mom's house on Friday after school so that they didn't know he was gone. He called me that night and said he was coming home. He thanked me for the scriptures because they had helped him. When he came home, he looked like death and smelled like it too. He went and took a shower, and then he went straight to the basement. I called Pastor Herman as he had asked to inform him that Al had made it home.

He said, "Can you try to keep him there until tomorrow? I'm coming over."

I said, "He has been up for days, so I don't think he's leaving to go anywhere."

I waited for a while before I went downstairs to speak to him because I knew he would be asleep.

Once I went downstairs, I asked, "What are you doing, Al? What are you thinking? Do you believe God can fix this?"

He didn't say a word. I forgot all about what I was going through. Not only did I have my kids to think about, but also I now had a drug-addicted husband.

As I began to leave to go upstairs, he asked, "Are you going to leave me? I cannot live without you and my girls."

I didn't respond. I just kept walking upstairs. Monday morning, I left to take the girls to school.

I said, "Go kiss Daddy good-bye."

They went down to the basement. I ran upstairs and went through his clothes. I got the credit card and the keys to his truck. I took the girls to school. Monday was my day off. I felt faint because I had not eaten in eight days. It felt like enzymes were eating away at my stomach. I started losing weight as if I had been smoking crack. As I returned home, Pastor Herman called and said that he would be over around one in the afternoon. I walked in and went to the basement. Al was knocked out.

As I walked upstairs, my mother called and asked, "Laina, are you all right?"

"Yes, ma'am, I'm going to call you right back."

I was trying to stay away from her because if she saw me, she would know that something was wrong.

"Al, get up. It's noon and Pastor Herman is coming to talk to you," I told him.

"I don't want to talk to him. I ain't ready to talk yet," he replied.

"Whether you want to talk or not, he will be here at one o'clock."

Around an hour later, my phone rang, and Pastor Herman was on the other end.

"Is he still there?" he asked.

I said, "Yes."

"I'm on my way."

We lived around the corner from the church. Pastor Herman pulled up along with one of the guys from the church. I opened the door, let them in, and told them he was downstairs. They went downstairs, and they were there for about forty minutes. Pastor Herman came up the stairs and called my name. I went to see what he wanted. He explained that because of the drugs, he had no choice but to let Al go from his job at the church. He said that he would pay Al for the next few weeks, and then he would work out a severance package and send us to counseling in Akron. After that, he told me he would determine what will happen next.

"I will stop the automatic deposits and give you the next few checks in your hand," he said.

Pastor Herman also explained that Al will be silenced because he was a leader at the church, which I totally understood. Being silenced means being removed from all duties as a leadership role while you receive counseling or until the pastor restores you back to the church. He had an affair, smoked crack, and may have a baby on the way. *He most definitely needs to be silenced*, I thought.

Later that day, I called to talk to Bishop and his wife because I had no one else to talk to, although Mona was there the whole time. I felt bad, because she was ready to have the baby soon, so I did not want to burden her. Honestly, she didn't know what to say or what to do. Al slept the rest of the day. On Tuesday, I headed back to work. Al said that we would go out and talk when I got off work. By this time, the rumors had begun to fly. Now all the leadership knew, including all the elders, ministers, deacons, and all of their wives. I was still trying to figure out what to do. I still hadn't eaten. I was managing twenty-six stylists, an eight-hundred-thousand-dollar salon, two kids, and a crack-addicted husband while trying not to lose my mind.

The phone started ringing off the hook. His family, his mother, and my family were all calling. His mother said that one of Al's friends had called her. He told her that Al had been fired because he had cheated on me and had three babies in the church. His friend Joe didn't even go to church, so how would he know anything? Al's mother was not someone I would share anything with. She was as messy as they came.

While we were on the phone, she was quietly laughing and asking, "Is it true?"

I politely told her, "If you have any questions regarding your son, you should direct them to him. I'll talk to you later. Have a nice day."

This day I did my hair, I did my make-up, and I got dressed really cute. I had on a new pair of wedge-heel sandals. I had to look my best because we were going to talk. Plus, I had to prove to myself that I still had it, because I was feeling low about everything that was going on. When I left work, I went straight home, because Al said that we would talk when I got there. As I arrived, I noticed that the truck was gone. He must have had another key, or maybe I was tired and left the key out.

"What the hell! Our marriage is at stake. Why would he leave and not call me?" I thought. Now I was frustrated. I have never been the type of woman to go and snoop around to check for stuff. I had never checked his cell phone or his pants pockets because I was not an insecure woman. I've never had to before. We trusted each other, but this time I needed to find out what was going on. I called his phone, and there was no answer. The more I called, the angrier I got. I drove around trying to locate him. I went past *The Church*, and there was no Al. I went by bars in the area, and there was no Al. I even drove around the old neighborhood where he used to get high. His parents lived on the next street over from Coath, so I drove by there.

I saw his father getting in his car, so I slowed down and tooted the horn. He walked over to my car.

He said, "Hey, you just missed Al around twenty to thirty minutes ago. He came by, and he said he lost his debit card. He asked if I could give him twenty-five dollars."

Al told him that he would give him the money back tomorrow.

I said, "Oh, okay."

I was not letting on to anything.

He asked, "Is everything all right?"

I said, "Yep, but I have to run. I'll see you later."

As I was about to pull off, Al's mother came to the screen door and said, "Hey, Laina, Al was over her a little while ago. He was acting real funny."

"Okay," I said, and then I pulled off.

I drove around the neighborhood a while longer, and I looked everywhere I thought he might be. My heart fell, because I just knew he wasn't over at Tiffany's house, but I began to fear the worse. I was filled with fear and anger all at the same time as I drove that way.

As I headed toward her house off of 93rd and Kinsman, I was praying out loud, "Lord, please don't let me see my truck over here."

The closer I got to her house, the slower I drove. My heart was racing, and my head was pounding. *"He is not going to be there. Al wouldn't do this"*, I thought. I was trying to rationalize this situation in my head, he has to much to loose, I had invested so much. By this time, I was so weary because I had not eaten or had any sleep in about two weeks. Lord please give me strength.

She lived two streets from the police station off 93rd and Kinsman.

As I crossed over Kinsman, my heart started pounding. There were two streets to go, and as I passed the next street, I slowed down. I had one street to go. Again I thought, *"Jesus, please don't let that truck be there.* " I didn't know what I was gonna do if I saw that my truck is over there. As I pulled to her street, I could see her house because she lived three houses from the corner on the left side. As I turned, I didn't see my truck.

"Thank you, Jesus!" I yelled.

She lived in the bottom level of a two-family house. Her upstairs neighbors were on the porch, looking down at me. They knew my car and who I was because I would go over her house regularly to check on her and the kids. I rode past the house slowly. I was relieved that I didn't see my truck. As I drove past the house, something on the inside said that I should turn around, so I did. As I came down at a different angle, I saw the top part of my truck parked in the back on the grass. *Oh my God!* So without hesitation, I pulled up in her driveway, and then I got out my car quietly.

The people upstairs must have known something.

"Aww, shit," I heard one of the men say.

I walked up the three stairs to the front porch. As I approached the front door, I began to listen, but I heard nothing except the people upstairs mumbling that it was about to go down. I noticed that the door was not shut all the way. Without thinking, I kicked the door open like Bruce Lee. When I walked in, he was sitting on the couch. She was sitting in the chair diagonally across from him and feeding her newborn.

I asked, "What the hell is going on?"

Al said, "Bae, listen, I'm just here talking about the baby. She is going to get an abortion."

"Mrs. Carpenter, I am so sorry--" she started to say.

I don't know what happened, but I blacked out and started swinging. The first lady had turned into a straight thug!

Al yelled, "Bae, come on! Let's go! The police are coming!"

His coward ass got up, ran out the house, and left us both in there. I continued punching her in the face, while she was still holding her baby.

She was trying to explain to me what was going on, while calling her oldest daughter who was seven at the time to come get the baby. I grabbed her by her hair and continued to whoop her butt!

I yelled, "You trifling bitch! You have the nerve to do this after all I did for you and your kids!"

Her daughter screamed, "Nana, Nana, you're hurting my mama!"

After I heard that, I snapped back, and although she was saying stuff, she never hit me back. In the midst of the struggle, my shoes came off. I heard the police sirens, and I could hear the upstairs neighbors saying the police were coming.

"Let me get out of here!" I said to myself. I would truly be going to jail tonight. I could only get one shoe on, and then I ran out the house. I got in my car and pulled off. I could not believe what I had just done, so out of my character. I must admit: it felt good. Afterward, I did not know where to go. I was scared to go home because I didn't know if she had really called the police to come to my house.

My phone rang, and it was Pastor Herman.

"Sister Carpenter, did you just go over Tiffany's house and fight her?"

"Yes, I did."

I had turned into a straight gangster. My mind was messed up. I had not eaten in two weeks.

He asked, "Where are you? Why did you do that? Do you know she said she called the police, and that her family is gang members and drug dealers? They are all on their way to her house. They said that they are coming to find you."

"So what!" I yelled.

"Where are you?" he asked again.

"None of your business!"

"My wife is out looking for you. She is upset. You've got her out here looking for you and risking her life and our baby's life," he said.

"Tell your pregnant-ass wife to go home!" I yelled before I hung up the phone.

As I continued to drive around I was all over the place, mentally and literally. I didn't know where I was. Around twenty minutes later, my phone rang again, and this time it was Bishop.

I answered, "Hello."

He said, "Daughter?"

I said, "Yes, sir."

He told me that Pastor Herman had just called him.

"Umm, Alaina, did you go over to that child's house, kick the door in, and then beat her in front of her kids?

With a strong voice, I said, "Yes, sir, I did."

He chuckled and asked, "Did you get her good?"

I said, "Bishop, I whooped her ass!"

Bishop was a very wise man, and he knew how to diffuse any situation.

He asked, "Where are you?"

I replied, "I don't know."

"Lord, have mercy she is in the 'hood and lost. Alaina, turn the car around and find a main street. I'm going to stay on the phone until you find your way back," he said.

"Thanks, Bishop."

"Do you need me to send Ma to the house?" Bishop asked.

"No, sir, I'm good."

"Pastor Herman said that his wife was out there looking for you, and she is in a high-risk pregnancy. I told him just leave Alaina Carpenter alone. You don't know how to handle her. She does not trust you or your wife. She is hurting. You have enough on your hands, dealing with Al. My wife and I will deal with Alaina."

I said, "Thank you, Bishop. I told Pastor Herman to tell his wife to leave me the hell alone!"

He asked, "You did?"

"Yes!" I said. "Bishop, they don't care about me. This is just for show."

"Good for you, Alaina!"

We both laughed.

I said, "I'm on Miles."

He said, "You know where you are now?"

"Yes, sir."

"Ok, call me when you get home, and let me know you made it home safely."

"Ok, Bishop."

"By the way, I don't believe that she is pregnant, and if she is, Al is not the father. Alaina, he was not in this alone," Bishop stated.

As I drove home, I could not stop reliving what had just happened, and what Bishop had just said. I finally made it home, and then I sat in my driveway and thought, *"What have I done?"* This was not me at all, and I felt horrible. As I walked in the house, the conviction fell on me so heavily that I began to weep. I walked to my room and fell to my knees because I was so broken. I did what I knew to do: I broke down and cried. As I continued to cry, I stretched out on my floor and began to pray to my Father.

"Lord, please forgive me--this hurts so bad. I am angry, confused, heartbroken I am literally sick to my stomach. I need you to help me and to give me the grace to go through this," I said.

I began to ask God to cover my girls and not allow this to scar them for life.

"Give me the wisdom to know how to tell them. Lord, I don't know what to do. I need you more than I have ever needed you before. Help me to push through."

The presence of God filled my room, and He began to lift the heavy burden that I was carrying. The peace of God began to flood my soul. It was an experience that I would never forget. I laid there and began to worship. I began to sing hymns from the old church that Bishop would sing.

"In thee oh Lord I put my trust

In thee oh Lord I put my trust

In thee oh Lord I put my trust

Be still and know that I am God

Be still and know that I am God

Be still and know that I am God"

After singing this, I went into my favorite hymn, "Great Is Thy Faithfulness."

"Great is thy faithfulness

Great is thy faithfulness, O God, my Father

There is no shadow of turning with thee

Thou changest not, thy compassions, they fail not

As thou hast been thou forever will be.

Great is thy faithfulness! Great is thy faithfulness!

Morning by morning new mercies I see

All I have needed thy hand hath provided;

Great is thy faithfulness, Lord, unto me!

Summer and winter and springtime and harvest,

Sun, moon and stars in their courses above

Join with all nature in manifold witness

To thy great faithfulness, mercy and love.

Pardon for sin and a peace that endureth.

Thy own dear presence to cheer and to guide;

Strength for today and bright hope for tomorrow,

Blessings all mine, with ten thousand beside!"

I could not stop there. I prayed *"Lord, have your way with me. Please, God, I cannot do this on my own."* I then began to sing these words:

"Have thine own way Lord

Have thine own way

You are the potter and I am the clay

Mold me and make me, after thine will

While I am waiting yielded and still

And then, I went back to "Great Is Thy Faithfulness."

By the time I got up from praying and worshiping it was after ten p.m. I had been down there for over three hours. I knew that if I was going to get through this, I was going to have many more nights like this. As I got up, I felt strength come upon me. I walked into my living room and sat on my couch, still feeling the presence of God. I knew I had to call Tiffany, and without reservation, I picked up my phone. I dialed *67 to block my phone number, and then I dialed her number.

She answered the phone, and said, "Hello."

I waited before saying anything, and so did she. It was as if she knew it was me, and she was waiting for my call.

I said, "Tiffany, I am so sorry."

She began to cry, and said, "No, I'm sorry. I understand why you did what you did. I deserved it and so much more. I can't believe I fell for this. You're the only mother I have, and I took my kids' nana away."

She could not stop apologizing and crying until I called her name.

"Tiffany, this is not all your fault. Al was more responsible, but that's not why I called you. I called to say that I am sorry and that I forgive you."

She just wept uncontrollably.

"Why are you apologizing to me? I should have never come to your house and did what I did in front of your kids," I said.

She said, "I explained to them that Mommy did something really bad to Nana. Please forgive me?"

"I already have" I replied. The phone was silent except for Tiffany sniffling.

"Tiffany, can I pray for you?"

She asked, "Pray for me? After what I've done to you? Oh my God, who are you?"

I began to pray and said, "Father, in the name of Jesus. I ask that you would touch Tiffany right now and let her know that you yet love her in spite of her actions. Help her to understand that this is why you died, for the sins of your people."

As I continued to pray for her, the same presence that had filled my room earlier now could be felt on the phone.

"Tiffany, God is here right now to forgive you if you want him to. You don't have to carry this pain. You keep saying that you are sorry to me, but you need to get it right with Him."

I lead her in a repentance prayer, and then we said amen. I told her that I loved her because I truly did. She informed me that she had my shoe.

I said, "Tiffany, you can throw it away because after this phone call you will probably never see me or talk to me again."

"Mrs. Carpenter, what about my kids? You're the only nana that they have--"

"You should have thought about that before you slept with my husband. Kiss the kids, and tell them I said I love them," I told her.

She continued to cry, and repeatedly said, "I am sorry. I'm sorry. I'm sorry."

I said, "Goodnight, Tiffany."

CHAPTER 5

Just Stand

Now the news had spread throughout the city. The largest church in the city was in a scandal. Now this was not the first scandal that this church had seen; however, it was the first one that was not swept under the rug. There were so many rumors. People who we thought loved us were running around adding more lies to this already horrific story. I worked in the mall, so it was filled with people daily. They would come in the salon, see me, and then begin to whisper. They would say things like, "That's Pastor Al's wife. She looks bad." It was so embarrassing. We were two weeks in at this time, but it seemed like two months.

The Sunday after I had found out everything, I could not face the people at the church. I went to my home church where Bishop was the pastor. I had planned to sit with my mom and my sister. They knew something was going on, but not because they had heard it from me. I was still confused and embarrassed. I had lost so much weight in this short period of time. It was about fifteen pounds in twelve days. As I walked in the church, my knees were shaking and my heart was skipping multiple beats. I stepped in the foyer, and I could sense the presence of God. I had not felt this feeling in a long time because God's presence didn't rest at the other church like this. That church was man- and flesh-driven. There was not a doubt in my mind that God was there to meet me.

The usher saw me, and said, "Lady Carpenter, it is so good to see you." We hugged. "Follow me."

At this church, if you were a pastor or pastor's wife, you would get special seating. Off to the front row I went. Now this felt weird, because when I was a member there, I used to seat other first ladies and clergy. Now I was being seated. I sat next to the assistant pastor's wife. The members were so happy to see me. I had been gone for three and a half years. I had only visited once or twice. Bishop and his wife were sitting in the pulpit. I locked eyes with him; we had a very unique connection. We could talk to each other without opening our mouths, and we knew exactly what we were saying to one another. Perhaps it was because we shared the same birth date.

He nodded his head and said, "I love you."

I nodded back. His wife could barely look up because her eyes were filled with tears. As the service went on, the presence of God was rich. I felt safe! It was a feeling I had not felt in three and a half years. I *never* felt safe at the other church, so I now basked in His presence again. It was so refreshing. Now it was the word of God time, and before Bishop got up to preach, he called for his eldest daughter to come and sing the sermonic solo. I knew that I was in for a treat because she could sing! She walked up to the altar, grabbed the microphone, looked at me, and then winked. I gave a half smile back at her.

As the musicians began to play, I thought, *"Oh no, not this song! If she sings this song, they are going to have to carry me out on a stretcher. I'm on the front row. This is not going to be pretty."*

They struck the chord, and she opened up her mouth and began to sing these words:

"What do you do when you've done all you can

And it seems like it's never enough?

And what do you say

When your friends turn away

And you all alone, alone?

Tell me, what do you give when you've given your all

And it seems like you can't make it through?

Well, you just stand when there's nothing left to do

You just stand, watch the Lord see you through

Yes, after you've done all you can,

You just stand

Tell me, how do you handle the guilt of your past?

Tell me, how do you deal with the shame?

And how can you smile while your heart has been broken

And filled with pain, filled with pain?

Tell me what do you give when you've given your all?

Seems like you can't make it through.

Child, you just stand when there's nothing left to do

You just stand, watch the Lord see you through

Yes, after you've done all you can,

You just stand

Stand and be sure

Be not entangled in that bondage again

BEHIND CHURCH DOORS

You just stand and endure

God has a purpose,

Yes, God has a plan

Tell me what do you do when you've done all you can

And it seems like you can't make it through?

Child, you just stand, you just stand, stand

Don't you dare give up through the storm,

Stand through the rain

Through the hurt,

Yeah, through the pain

Don't you bow, and don't you bend

Don't give up, no, don't give in

Hold on,

Just be strong,

God will step in

And it won't be long

After you've done all you can, after you've done all you can

After you've gone through the hurt,

After you've gone through the pain

After you've gone through the storm,

After you've gone through the rain

Prayed and cried,

Prayed and cried

Prayed and cried

Prayed and cried, oh my

After you done all you can you just stand!"

After she sang, I was filled with grief and strength all at the same time. The pain was so heavy, but she sang strength into my soul. I tried to keep it together, but I couldn't. By the fourth word, I was on my feet, and the tears began to flow like Niagara Falls. I knew that God was giving me instructions through this song.

At the end of the song, she kept singing my name. *Alaina, after you've done all you can. You prayed and cried, Laina you prayed and cried. Alaina stand.*

I thought, *"Don't you call my name again because I can't handle this."* As I glanced into the pulpit at Bishop and his wife, she was red as a tomato. She had her monogramed, laced handkerchief covering her whole face. Bishop and I locked eyes again, and it was a wrap. My weak legs buckled from underneath me, and to the floor I went.

Bam! I had tried as long as I could to keep it together. As I hit the floor, I was in a fetal position, and I cried like a baby. While I was lying there, I zoned out. I didn't know what was going on around me. It was as if God had shut everything out to get my attention. He showed me so many things while I was lying there. He took me back four weeks, to the end of March. I had accompanied Bishop's wife to Washington, DC, for a women's conference. This particular night, Evangelist Wanda Frazier Parker was preaching, and she was a powerhouse! While she was in the midst of ministering, she stopped and began to listen as if someone was giving her instruction. She stopped completely in her tracks and began to weep. I thought, *"Oh boy, what's going on?"* I felt strange on the inside, but I didn't understand why.

She finally broke her silence and said, "Oh my God, there is someone here tonight who in the next two to three weeks your life is going to change. It will be nothing that you were expecting. You will receive some bad news. It will be the most devastating news that you have ever received. The pain that you are going to have will seem almost unbearable. The life that you have known will be no more. God said that he will give you the strength that you need to go through. There's one rule: you can't quit. I wish I could show you what's waiting on the other side of this. Your future is so big and bright. You are going to be blessed beyond your wildest dreams, beyond your imagination, but you can't quit!"

Because I was a guest of the Bishop's wife, I was seated on the front row. She was sitting in the pulpit facing me.

As the speaker continued to give this death sentence of a prophecy, I sat there feeling like Judas in Matthew 26:25 when Judas said, *"Master is it I?"*

Jesus said, "You have answered correctly."

I knew that she was speaking to me. I glanced up at the pulpit at Bishop's wife, and she was looking back at me because she knew as well!

Evangelist Parker made an altar call and said, "If you think that God is talking to you, come to the altar."

I thought, *"Who in the world would want to come for that death sentence? But the altar was full."* I never moved because I was on the front row.

I lifted my hands up to God in a surrendered posture and said, "Yes, Lord."

I began to weep, and so did Evangelist Parker.

As I lay out on the floor, I saw bright lights. I heard a voice saying, *I will never leave you or forsake you*. While it was like an out-of-body experience, I guess the altar workers were trying to get me up.

The first thing I heard was Bishop saying, "Leave her alone! God is speaking to her."

When I finally came to, the first face I saw was my mom. I grabbed her, and we cried and cried. She held me in her arms. My sister DeeDee was next. We hugged, and the line of support grew to well over fifteen people. They began to pray for me.

Bishop said, "Well, there is nothing else to do. God has done what He wanted to do here today."

Then he opened the altar up for prayer. People came from everywhere. Bishop laid hands on people, and they were healed. God truly used His daughter that day in order to pour strength into me for the days ahead!

THE DANGER OF LEAVING PREMATURALLY

It felt good to be back in the company of Bishop and his wife. Before leaving and joining the other church, Al and I had served together in ministry with Bishop for almost fourteen years. I had been there a year prior to marrying Al. We were very close to Bishop and his family. He had been like a father to me after my father had died, and his wife had been more like a sister to me. Bishop had trained us both in the ministry. They were the godparents to our children. We had done a lot together, including vacations, holidays, dinners, shopping sprees, and the list could go on. Bishop was the chaplain for the police department, and Al was his assistant. They were like father and son. They were complete opposites of each other, but they were what each other needed. Al had needed a father who could teach him how to be a godly and responsible man, and Bishop had needed a son who wanted to be taught and to help him not to be so uptight. Al and Bishop were a perfect match!

BEHIND CHURCH DOORS

I would stayed at the house and watched their two daughters every week while his wife finished her bachelor's degree. Bishop and his wife did not trust many people in their home, but they trusted us. Our relationship extended far beyond the church walls. We were family, and everyone knew it. We paid a price to be that close to leadership. When Al decided that he wanted to take his family from this church, it was devastating not just for our family but also for Bishop's family as well. Bishop said anybody could have left the church but not us. He took our leaving very personally. Bishop did not understand, and neither did I.

Al wanted to leave because our church was a strict Pentecostal church that was not community friendly. It had the reputation of being very exclusive and snobby. You had to dress a certain way or be looked down on. Al was from the inner city, and nothing about him was stuffy or exclusive. He wanted to go back and help the people where he came from. Although I agreed with Al about how the church was, I didn't want to leave just yet. We were safe there! The strict lifestyle and holiness living kept Al clean for thirteen and a half years while under Bishop's leadership. I was able to deal with the rules, but I would not have been able to deal with the drugs. Bishop never took the time to understand Al's giftings or his anointing. Instead, he forced Al to become his clone and that frustrated Al. Al wanted to be himself and who he believed God called him to be with Bishop's understanding and his blessing. The whole clergy collar and wearing black all the time was not Al. These limitations robbed both men of reaching their full potential of who they were supposed to be in each other's lives.

Al was a phenomenal basketball player. He was a conference MVP, an all-state performer, and just an all-around beast known as the "Ice Man" in the city of Cleveland. Al had started, and I assisted, a mentoring program in the city called Athletes for Christ in 1994. Al used basketball as a platform to draw inner-city male youths and to empower them with tools to stay free from drugs and alcohol. This was what destroyed his basketball career, because of personal bad choices and even worse influences by some of his siblings. Al was the youngest of six brothers.

ALAINA HOLLOWAY-CARPENTER

Although Al was raised in a two parent home, his father was an alcoholic, and his mother was very controlling and not supportive at all. His father attended every game while intoxicated however his mother never showed up at any of his games. When he came home and told her how many points, steals, or rebounds he made she would reply, "That's all?" This made Al go out and score more points. He made the front page of the local newspaper regularly, but it never impressed his mom. Nothing Al did was ever good enough for her. All he ever wanted to do was please his mom. He was a full-fledged alcoholic by middle school, and during his freshman year of high school, he was not able to function playing ball without a drink. But even as an alcoholic, he was still breaking every record in the city.

After graduating from high school, he attended the University of North Dakota, where he continued to drink and break records. By this time, it began to take a toll on him. He tried cocaine while there. After his third year at University of North Dakota, Al lost two of his brothers within six months of each other. That, ultimately, brought him back to the streets of Cleveland. His alcoholism led him to try crack cocaine one time, and he was hooked. Al always regretted the day he went to get drugs with Ray, a fifteen-year-old drug dealer who was shot three times in the back of the head while making a drug transaction. He was so hurt because he could not bring Ray back, as well as angry that he had not made it to the NBA. That is why he'd started AFC, to help the youth make better choices and to save other Rays.

Now Al was living a drug-free life, and he was able to help so many youths in the city. He had a two-day tournament that consisted of a pep rally with singers, rappers, and dancers. Before they were able to play, the youth had to attend a breakaway meeting. This is where they received the instructions on how to live and play drug and alcohol-free and that only was through Jesus Christ. One year, there were over one hundred and fifty young men who'd made that commitment. All you could see on the court were white tees and hands lifted. This was a powerful movement, and Al believed this is what God had called him to do, and so did I.

Bishop believed that if the church was having an event, your first priority should be to what was going on there, no matter what. We had even been advised back then that we could not go to the movies on church nights if you were a leader. Al and I had organized our second annual One Way to Play Drug Free tournament and rally. We had our permits and everything. The church put something on the calendar at the last minute, but we continued on with our plans. We had already paid for the stage, trophies, and the food. Bishop was not happy at all. What made matters worse was the youth at the church wanted to come to our event. They were tired of being in church all day because it was boring to them. There was nothing for the youth to do at that time.

Bishop put out the decree that no youth could participate in our event. He demanded that they attend what he planned. I was hurt, but I knew the rules. Our event was amazing. It was the best one that he had done thus far. Not only did one hundred and fifty players give their lives to Christ, but so did their coaches and some of the parents that were in attendance. Drug dealers were coming over to give Al money to help pay for Gatorade and to ask Al to pray for them. They had witnessed the change in Al and thought if God could it for him then maybe it was hope for them. Al and I were pumped up, we believed that this is what God had called us to do, even though we did not have the support of our leaders and church family (They never supported anything we did unless it was beneficial to them.) The next day we were still on a high as we went to church. Some of the people seemed a little standoffish toward us. We asked ourselves, *"What is happening?"*

The youth were almost afraid to talk to us. You had to be a member to know what was going on. If you did not follow the rules, you would be ostracized. I told Al that Bishop must have said something to the leaders and the youth at the event the day before.

Al said, "So what? We did what God told us to do."

It was time for Bishop to preach.

As he stood there, he looked at the crowd from behind his circled wired frame glasses and said, "Before I preach, I have an announcement to make, as long as I am the pastor of this church and we call a meeting and you are a leader, you will be in attendance, or you will not lead here!"

Bishop was known to use the pulpit as his boxing ring. He would get you told, curse you out, and tell all your business, all on a Sunday morning. You couldn't fight back. When he had gone into his sermon, without singing one note of a hymn, which is what he did every Sunday. The church knew he was mad as hell, and many were scared but not me and Al. We were still excited about what had taken place on the court. Bishop was able to tell by the look on my face that I was not moved by his announcement. I was tired of being controlled, bullied and bible bashed for having my own opinion.

No pants, no make-up, no big earrings, no haircuts for women, no prom, no homecoming or school dances, no R & B music, no sororities or fraternities--he had a scripture for each one of these, even though they had been taken out of context. Our whole lives were being controlled by man-made rules. These rules had absolutely nothing to do with our salvation nor was he and members of his family following these rules. In the midst of his sermon, he began to go off. He was angry and full of rage while he preached. He said that God was only saving souls on the altar and the youth should have been tarrying for the Holy Ghost, not trying to run to a basketball court.

He began to mock basketball and said, "Ain't nobody getting saved on a basketball court, no how."

His words were filled with venom, and everyone could feel it including Al. I was so mad. I thought "more people had gotten saved on the basketball court than on this altar!" Al's countenance dropped on his face. He looked as if to ask himself, *why would the man I loved and admired, and whom I serve be attacking me like this?*

Al had never been the same from that day to this one. I believed in my heart that Al had relapsed that day. It had just taken five years for it to manifest. I could not believe that Bishop had done that. I had seen him humiliate a lot of people, but I just never thought he would have done it to us. I didn't speak to Bishop for over a week. I hadn't watched the kids, and Al hadn't ridden with him for police duty. We were done!

After everything died down, Bishop invited us over to talk. He tried to explain why he did what he did. He felt that he was right and had never thought he should be challenged. Our opinion never mattered and back then he never apologized. He was always right. He told us that he was working on something big for us. He couldn't tell us right then, but he said he would stay in touch. About a month later, Bishop called me over to the house.

He asked, "How is Al as a husband and a father? I know how he is as a son and a preacher."

"Bishop, why are you asking me this?"

"Alaina, you can't say anything to Al," Bishop replied.

I was confused. I wondered, *"What is going on?"* He explained that there was a church in Youngstown, Ohio, that was in need of a pastor.

He said, "I'm thinking about sending you and Al."

I said, "Bishop, I am not going to Youngstown."

"So you will tell God no?" he asked.

I responded, "God didn't tell us to go; you did."

"Alaina, God is speaking through me," he said.

We had been brainwashed that God speaks through the leader and the leader speaks to us. That was just like hearing from God. He always said that he held our gifts in his hands. Although I'd never read this in the Bible, I trusted him, so I quieted down. I told Bishop that the same Al you saw at church was the same Al that he was at home. He loves me and his kids. He brought his check home every week and put it in my hands. He is up every morning at six a.m. and praying sometimes almost for two hours. He is truly a godly man. He isn't perfect, but he has been a good man.

Bishop explained that he shared this with his wife, and she was not in agreement with it at all. I was her only real friend at the church and in the city. They were not from Cleveland and she was not outgoing. She was extremely shy. She was losing so much more than just a member....a trusted friend. I had never seen them disagree publicly. She was really upset.

He said, "I need to move fast because the holy convocation is in six weeks. I want to make the announcement then."

I responded, "Bishop, that's too fast."

He'd said, "It's just an announcement. You won't actually go until next year."

I truly believe that Bishop only did this to try and make up for what had done to us in the pulpit. The only problem was we didn't believe God had called us to pastor. Just because you can preach and teach does not mean that you have been called to pastor. However, because we trusted and was loyal to Bishop, we went to Youngstown, Ohio, to pastor the church even though we knew we were not called. We were in an unfamiliar city, and we didn't know anyone. My sister and her family came with us. We had to drive every Sunday and every Wednesday for an hour and forty minutes, and in the winter even longer, until we sold our home so we could move closer. We stayed there for a year until we weren't able to take it anymore. The former pastor was still a member of the church, and although she stepped down, she did not want to relinquish her pastorship. She felt that because we were young, she would be able control us. When she realized that was not happening, she tried to make it unbearable for us to stay. It was not worth it for my children and I to be subjected to this hostility.

I called Bishop to let him know what was going on, and he agreed that we should come home. While we had been there for that year, we paid off the church and the apartment building that they owned. We returned to Cleveland a year later. Al felt as if he had disappointed Bishop and that he had failed him. Al carried that guilt of disappointing flesh with him. He had done this even though he'd known we weren't supposed to pastor. He had not been able to stand up to Bishop. Even when he tried, Bishop would shut him down by backing up whatever he was saying with scriptures that would fit his logic. If we had never been made to go to Youngstown, we would have never ended up at the next church.

This reminds me of the story of Saul, David and Goliath. When David went to fight Goliath, all he had on was a tunic, and he had his shepherd's staff. Saul did not believe that David would be successful in the fight with just that, so Saul redressed David. He tried to make David look and function like him, and it did not work.

Bishop had done the same thing. The leaders had to wear all black on a regular basis with their clergy collars, in and out of church. He said that this was a sign of total surrender to the call of the gospel of Jesus Christ and to leadership. For the leaders to wear their regular clothes was a treat.

In 1 Samuel 17:38-40, the Bible says, *"Then Saul gave David his own armor--a bronze helmet and a coat of mail. David put it on, strapped the sword over it, and took a step or two to see what it was like, for he had never worn such things before." "I can't go in these,' he protested to Saul. 'I'm not used to them.' So David took them off again. He picked up five smooth stones from a stream and put them into his shepherd's bag. Then, armed only with his shepherd's staff and sling, he started across the valley to fight the Philistine and ultimately defeated Goliath."*

The difference between Al and David is that David removed Saul's armor while Al kept the Bishop's armor on and completely lost his identity. Al joining the new church was a breath of fresh air and freedom, or so it appeared.

Now I know you who are reading this book are probably wondering why we stayed here and suffered this abuse. I had three reasons:

It was safe for us. Al was staying off of drugs in this ministry.

I truly loved Bishop and his family.

We were conditioned to it. If you didn't follow the rules, you would be alienated or embarrassed publicly.

He believed the scripture in 1 Timothy 5:20: *"Publicly rebuke those who sin, so that the rest will also be afraid"* (HCSB). The head of our deacon board who had held this position for years decided to allow his daughter to attend her senior prom. He was not hiding it at all. He told Bishop that he was going to allow his daughter to go, regardless of the consequences. He tried to understand why this was such a closed case.

Again, on a Sunday morning as Bishop was about to preach, he stated, "I am going to say this one time and one time only. If you are a leader in this church and you allow your children to go to prom, you will be publicly silenced. The Bible says in 1 John 2:15, *"Do not love the world not the things in the world. If anyone loves the world, the love of the father is not in him."* He also believed that prom night is where you would lose your virginity.

I never agreed with this. I went to prom and did not lose my virginity that night. My date took me to prom, and after prom he brought me home. (I had lost my virginity months prior to that night). Not only did the deacon and his wife allow their daughter to go, he escorted her as well for she was the senior prom queen. The next Sunday just as Bishop promised, the man was publicly disciplined and relieved of all his duties. The deacon was such a stand-up man. He was a class act. He never argued publicly. He took his punishment, and a week or so later, he removed his family from the church, never to return again. What a loss.

This consistent behavior caused those of us who remained to become afraid, and we just went along with the program and followed the rules. We often question why abused women stay with their abusers, but we do the same thing in this type of situation. We stay in a church where we have been abused spiritually, emotionally, and sometimes financially. We complain and talk about the leadership among ourselves, but we continue to go back week after week, thinking that it is going to change. The difference between the two is that the abused woman knows that she is being abused; however, we in the church have no idea of what's going on. It becomes normal until you leave and look back. We must remember the old engineering adage concerning laying a train track.

The error starts when the engineer is only one degree off, which seems small at first, yet a hundred miles down the road is when the error is apparent.

Jesus and His apostles warned their followers in one form or another to "be not deceived" in regards to false teaching or teachers--understanding that they were speaking to believers, not unbelievers or even new believers, but established Christians.

Families are being destroyed on a weekly basis, and it is not all the pastors' faults. We have to bear some responsibility. You see, many of us mistake our emotions for a leading of the spirit of God. We are so heavenly minded that we are no earthly good. We refuse to study the Word of God for ourselves or to gain an understanding of it. Some leaders prey on the inability of this behavior. They want us to depend and believe what they say so that they will never be challenged. The Bible compels us to honor our pastors.

Hebrews 13:17 (ESV)--*"Obey your leaders and submit to them, for they are keeping watch over your souls, as those who will have to give an account. Let them do this with joy and not with groaning, for that would be of no advantage to you";*

1 Timothy 5:17--*"Elders who do their work well should be respected and paid well, especially those who work hard at both preaching and teaching";*

1 Thessalonians 5:12--*"Dear brothers and sisters, honor those who are your leaders in the Lord's work. They work hard among you and give you spiritual guidance."* It is scriptures like these, that have believers and the leaders confused about boundaries; and

Ephesians 4:8-13--*"Wherefore he saith, When he ascended up on high, he led captivity captive, and gave gifts unto men. Now that he ascended, what is it but that he also descended first into the lower parts of the earth? He that descended is the same also that ascended up far above all heavens, that he might fill all things. And he gave some, apostles; and some, prophets; and some, evangelists; and some, pastors and teachers. For the perfecting of the saints, for the work of the ministry, for the edifying of the body of Christ."*

God never told Al nor myself that He had called us to pastor. Man (flesh) told us that He did.

Question? What do you do when God gives you an assignment, but your leader tells you that God didn't call you to do that, that he called you for something else?

So many people were affected by our move. We were very active there. Al was one of the assistant pastors. He was also over the evangelism department as well as the drug ministry. I sang on the praise team and in the choir. I also helped reestablish the praise dance ministry, and I served his wife with everything she had going on from her house to the church. I was like her armor-bearer, without the title. Together Al and I were assistant youth leaders on the national level of our church reformation. We also would volunteer and clean the church every week.

Al was always called upon by Bishop to preach regularly. Bishop did not play when it came to who he allowed to preach in his pulpit, especially on Sundays and holidays. Our church was known for bringing in big-name preachers from all over the country. Al was a phenomenal preacher and teacher. Bishop would allow Al to preach on Sundays and holidays. Some of the other ministers hated it. They would say that Al was Bishop's favorite. Bishop had been diagnosed with cancer, and there were some other things that were going on in his personal life that he had been accused of. There were accusations that tested his family and his faith. I had never seen him so low.

It was the week before Mother's Day, and Bishop called Al, and said, "I need you to preach on Sunday."

Al was so shocked because Bishop would never give away a Sunday like that unless it was a preacher from out of state. His instructions to Al were to preach Jesus. Bishop was the only person who would call Al by his full name.

"Albert Eugene Carpenter, your spiritual father needs a word!" he said with conviction.

Al began preparing for the Mother's Day sermon. He and I prayed and fasted all week. We knew how important it was. Sunday came, and it was time for the word. The church was packed. You know the CME saints were all in attendance (these were people who only come to the church on Christmas, Mother's Day, and Easter). Bishop was so broken. I had never seen him like this nor had the members of our congregation. It appeared as if he was giving up.

After the sermonic solo, Al got up and walked to the pulpit and began to pray. This man prayed to the point that I believe the angels had come down from heaven. When he was done, he said, turn your Bibles to Luke 8, 43-48, and his subject on Mother's Day was "Bow Down." Al preached as if God had a gun on him. The power of God came in that place. I had never seen Bishop lose his composure like that. He was known to cry and to do his dance, but to totally lose it? Never! At one point, he was stretched out on the floor in the pulpit, and so was everyone else in the church. Pastor Gwen McCurry and Al begin to pray for Bishop until God restored hope, peace, and strength back into him. After service was dismissed, people were still on the floor and on the altar. What a service!

We were very instrumental in the ministry, so for us to leave with no warning was devastating for all of us. Although we were not at the same church, I thought we would still have a relationship with Bishop and his wife. My girls and I felt like they had abandoned us, because the relationship stopped completely, and I guess they felt like we had abandoned them. To be back with them felt like old times.

Although I did not not want to move to *The Church* I didn't want to stay there either. I began to feel like I was being used. I would do the Bishop's wife hair free every week and sometimes their daughters hair as well. I would get new clothes here and there and some paid overnight stays here and there. I was told it was a honor to serve the first family. So I did. I believed that God would bless me by doing this. One day I shared a dream that I had with the Bishop's wife. I explained that God gave me a sermon that I think He wanted me to preach. I was not a minister at this time. Although I knew I had been called, the Bishop had not allowed me to start the ministerial class so I just sang on the praise team and in the choir. Bishop only looked at Al as the preacher. So I was a little hesitant to share but because she was my friend I shared. I began to tell her with passion that it came from Genesis 29. I stated that the title of my sermon was entitled the Leah Syndrome.

Jacob, fleeing the wrath of his brother, Esau, married both daughters of his uncle Laban. But his marriage to the elder sister, Leah, came not by choice but by trickery.

Leah, the pawn in someone else's trickery, must live out her life married to a man who did not love her, did not choose her, and did not want her. Every day she faced the fact that her husband loved her younger sister, not her.

Rachel, the younger sister, appeared to have everything going for her except her ability to bear children. Leah, her older sister, seemed to have no problem getting pregnant. Every day for more than a decade she heard the sound of her sister's children outside her tent, and she yearned for a child of her own.

The rivalry between the two sisters existed because each one wanted what the other had.

Leah wanted Jacob's love, expressed in the naming of her sons:

"Now therefore my husband will love me" after firstborn Reuben's birth.

"Because the Lord has heard that I am unloved. He has therefore given me this son also" after Simeon's birth.

"Now this time my husband will become attached to me, because I have borne him three sons" after Levi's birth.

"Now I will praise the Lord" after Judah's birth.

"God has given me my hire, because I have given my maid to my husband" after Issachar's birth.

"God has endowed me with a good endowment; now my husband will dwell with me, because I have borne him six sons" after Zebulun's birth.

Rachel conceived only when "the Lord opened her womb," not before. Her envy of Leah in no way changed her barrenness. It merely made her miserable.

Leah had to find contentment in the sons she bore. Her marriage did not change. Jacob loved Rachel most, even at the end of her life. When preparing to meet Esau and his 400 men, Jacob put the maids and their children first in line, then Leah and her children second, and Rachel and Joseph as far back as possible to protect them. Leah never knew the affection from Jacob that she yearned for.

I was so full, I literally was preaching it to her and she was interjecting while I was doing so with moans and grunts and religious lingo such as "Girl this will PREACH!" I see where you are going with this, I looked at her and said... "all at the Hands of their father who favored Rachel. How does it feel to be Leah when your own Father looks at you and call you unattractive?" As I was preaching this to her she is like OMG! Alaina this is good. When I finished she was in disbelief and said "WOW are you sure He told you to preach this?" It was like someone had stuck a straight pin into a balloon and the air sizzled out. I said maybe He didn't. I was crushed because she refused to see the gift in me. A few weeks later it was women's day and the Bishops wife was to preach. We were all so excited she was new to preaching and at times very nervous. After our one hundred voice women's choir in white was finished singing our A &B selection we sat down and I was on the front row. The Bishop got up to to introduce the women's day speaker as his best friend, and the mother of his children his wife. We were all screaming and encouraging her because we knew this was not her comfort zone. I was the loudest, cheering her on and praying for her all at the same time. She quieted us down and as we took our seats she asked us to open our bibles and turned to Genesis 29. I thought I know she is not about to preach what I think she is. She read the scripture with a quivering voice after she finished she said the title of my sermon will be the Leah Syndrome she looked at me and winked her eye. You could have bought me for ten cents. She didn't even change the title nor the content, she preached it just like I gave it to her. I knew then that this friendship was one sided. It was always about her and her only. I never said anything to her about it nor did I share any more dreams or sermons with her and because I never said anything this behavior continued in many other instances and with many other women in the church. No one ever told her the truth. If you did you were going to have to face her husband, and that was not going to be good. Several people tried to talk to them and as a result they were punished severely. They were the topic in his sermons, discussed at leadership meetings, removed from their positions with no questions asked, and blackballed by the church and reformation. I even witnessed people and families excommunicated from the church by way of a letter, and then exposed on the next Sunday by reading the letters over the pulpit. This was all because they had their own opinion or didn't agree with something he or a family member said.

When it came to Bishop's immediate family the rules were changed and altered. If a members child got pregnant before marriage they would be silenced and not be able to participate in any church function. When his children got pregnant, they continued in ministry with only a written public apology. Our kids could not attend high school dances or proms while his children quietly attended homecoming dances and prom. Talk about a double standard, he preached against sororities and fraternities while the Bishop serves as a 33rd degree mason. This behavior made his children feel that they were superior to the standard that he set for everyone else which caused contention amongst the youth and other members of the church. This could be a book all by itself. The saddest part of all of this is that they believed that everyone was jealous of what they had, who they were, and who they were connected to. When in fact several people felt sorry for them. I personally felt sorry for their children because I saw first hand that the reason they had the best of everything (the newest gadget, the finest clothes, the best education) was mostly to satisfy and fill the void of their parents not being fully present. They were always fulfilling their ministerial duties and not being there for their children.

CHAPTER 6

Lights, Camera, Action

By now, word had gotten back to Pastor Herman that I had gone back to my old church with Bishop on that Sunday. Pastor Herman knew Al did not go with me. Monday morning I received a phone call saying that Pastor Herman wanted to see us. In this meeting were Pastor Herman, Lady Herman, Al, and me. He was a little irritated in his tone toward me. I assumed it was because of my visit to my old church on Sunday, but I did not care. He began to explain that because of Al's position in the church, he had to publicly discipline him for his sins. Now, because of what had happened to me the day before, I was ready for anything. Pastor Herman explained that he would not do it on a Sunday morning. He said, instead, he would do it on Wednesday at Bible study night. I thought it would be better on a Wednesday, because on Sunday, we were having three services. If he did it on a Sunday, it would have had to be done at each service, whereas on a Wednesday night, only one time. He explained how he would do it. He said he would not expose the sin and that it would be short. Then he asked me if I would accompany Al in front of the people for the public discipline.

I said, "Absolutely not, because these are his sins and not mine. I did nothing, but I will come and support him."

He said, "If you stand with him, it will be a united front, and the people will be encouraged by your union."

I thought, *"This man is crazy as hell. This man is trying to humiliate me on this stage too."*

Lady Herman asked, "Sister Carpenter, are you gonna bring your girls?"

I just looked at her and gave her a look that could kill.

"No, I will not," I said.

"Sister Carpenter, we believe that God is going to turn this around. It will be good for your girls to take part so that the members can see God move in your family's life."

Why in the hell is this woman offering me any advice? I never asked her for anything since I've been here, so why would she think I wanted it now?

"No, they will not be in attendance. I'm not changing my mind. I barely even want to be there. So can we change the subject, please?"

We left the office, scared to death. This was a mega ministry, and although it was not going to be on a Sunday, Wednesday night Bible study still had a strong attendance of at least seven to eight hundred people.

Al said, "Alaina, we're going to get through this."

I replied, "I know."

From that time to the following Wednesday, which seemed like an eternity, I was sick to my stomach. I was steadily losing weight. I went from a size 14/16 to a size 8 in three and a half weeks. Wednesday was finally here; that morning I spoke to Bishop and his wife. She asked me what I had decided to do. She wanted to know if I was going on the stage with Al or not. I decided at that moment I would go. I did not want the devil or anyone else to feel that they had won. If we were going to fight for our marriage, we were going to fight together.

Bishop's wife said, "You are better than me, because I couldn't do it." I didn't understand why she said that when we are taught that God wants us to reconcile. Now here I was, faced with adversity, and I was trying to live it the way God wanted me to, and she said that. Even if she felt it, why would she say it?

"We will be praying for you," she said.

It got close to the time to go, and I began to get ready. I got sharp on purpose. I did my hair, I did my make-up to perfection, and I threw on a black-and-cream-colored wide-legged pants suit, with my nails freshly manicured.

They were never going to catch me off.

I said, "Al, come here."

When I looked at him, he appeared to be lifeless. I could not think about what I was going through because my best friend was a dead man walking.

I said, "Look at me. This is probably the hardest thing we have ever had to face as a team, but we're going to get through this. I got you. Al, do you remember when we got married? The only advice that my mom gave us was that there is no such thing as a fifty-fifty in a relationship. It's one hundred to zero. Meaning that some days you will give one hundred, and I will have nothing, or I will give seventy, and you will give thirty, and so on."

As I looked into his eyes, I said, "This is the day I will give one hundred."

He looked and me and said, "How can you be so strong and love me like this after what I've done to you?"

I said, "This is nobody but God."

I could still hear Bishop's daughter singing, *Alaina, stand*. I prayed for us as he lay in my arms.

He said, "Alaina, I am so sorry. Bae, we're going to make it."

I responded, "I know."

As we prepared to leave, my phone rang, and again it was Bishop and his wife. He asked to speak to Al, and to this day, I do not know what he said to him. I just knew we were going to see them on the upcoming Saturday at his house.

Al gave me back the phone. Bishop said, "Me and Ma are praying for you. You can do this. I am so proud of you, Alaina. You're more woman than most."

I said, "Thank you, Bishop. I love you." Now that was what I needed to hear.

As we left for Bible study, my stomach began to knot up. I did not know what to expect. I had all kinds of thoughts going on. As we approached the church, I could not help but notice all the cars that were there. Bible study was always packed but not like this.

I said, "Al, is there a league playing ball here tonight?"

The Church was a sports complex as well. It was known for having soccer and basketball leagues.

Al said, "Not to my knowledge."

We parked the car and got out. We held hands, and both of ours were sweaty. I believe Al was just as scared as I was. When we walked into the church, it was packed.

"Oh my."

We went to go sit down, and some of the leaders of *The Church* came to greet us. All eyes were on me. I could feel them looking at me from all angles. I asked myself, *"Why the hell are they looking at me so hard and intense? If they think I'm going to break down, they've got another thing coming. I would never give them the opportunity to see me vulnerable. Ok, Holy Ghost, please kick in."*

More people began to come in. *My God, where are all these people coming from?* I believe *The Church* held twenty-five hundred people, and every seat was taken, along with people standing in the back,. They had to bring more chairs in and add them down the sides of each row. *Did someone do a phone a tree?* (I later found out that is exactly what Pastor Herman had done. It was a new phone system that they had implemented a few months prior. He had called every member to invite them to come out to the service. On the recording, he said, "Don't miss service on Wednesday. Pastor has something really important to say."

As I looked at Al, it seemed as if he was about to pass out. I gently grabbed his hand, and he grabbed mine back.

I said, "I've got you."

He said, "I love you."

I thought, *Wait a minute, this is my husband, not my boyfriend.* We had been together since I was sixteen years old. We had two beautiful children together and had built a comfortable life. I had to shake myself, and I thought, *"Hell no! I will not let the devil come in and destroy this union."* The Bible says, "Who God put together, let no man put asunder."

As I sat there, my faith and my strength began to build. I kept looking at all the people's faces. I was then reminded that in Jeremiah 1:8, the Bible says, *"Don't be afraid of the people for I will be with you and protect you. I the Lord have spoken."* Well, that was just what I needed. It was standing room only in this church. They were all there to see what was going to happen. Some of the people that were in attendance knew what had happened, and some did not.

After praise and worship, Pastor Herman took the stage, and he began to pace back and forth.

He said, "This is so hard. I hate I've got to do this, but I've got to do it. Some of the leaders yelled out "pastor you can do it, we praying for you". "Come here, Al." he stated.

I released his hand, and Al walked to the stage.

Lady Herman looked at me and asked, "Are you going?"

I walked up to the stage with him. The only reason I didn't move at first was because he'd called Al and not me. As we walked up the stairs to get to the stage, I grabbed Al's hand again.

Pastor Herman began to say that Al had been the best executive pastor ever.

He said, "When I was down and felt like giving up, it was Al who would come and pray for me."

As I looked at the audience, it was very tense because some of the people had no idea what was going on. *"Are they about to leave The Church?"* There were many looks of confusion. Pastor Herman continued to go on and say that Al had been caught in a moral failure. That was a bold-faced lie. Al didn't get caught in anything because he told on himself.

The audience gasped for air as someone yelled out, "Oh my God."

Pastor Herman continued and said, "Al is no longer Pastor Al in this church. He is now Brother Al. I am taking him down publicly. He will no longer be on paid staff I repeat he is Brother Al. The church will pay him for the next two weeks, and we are going to work out a severance package." I believe that the only reason that he had to repeat that he was Brother Al and not Pastor Al was because he knew how much the members loved him and he wanted to be clear that there was only one pastor at this church.

He continued to talk about Al being a good man, but that he just got caught up. Al could not handle it. He lost it. He began to cry uncontrollably in front of all those people. I did not shed one tear. I put my hand on Al's back, and I began to speak with other tongues to intercede for my husband. Pastor Herman kept talking, but I didn't hear anything else he said. I went into a realm in God that I had not been in for a long time.

The next thing I knew Pastor Herman came over. He grabbed, hugged, and began to pray for Al never acknowledging me at all. They both fell to the floor. I began to pray for them both. They looked ridiculous down there, rolling on the floor.

When they finally got up from the floor, Pastor Herman saw that I was standing there looking at them both he finally commented and says and his lovely wife stands by his side, we will keep them both in prayer. Some of the people in the audience began to clap for me. I believe Pastor Herman got upset because I didn't shed a tear. It's almost as if he was putting on a show that I was not going to participate in. I believe Al had been drinking prior to the stage so that he would be able to handle the humiliation and embarrassment we were about to endure.

Pastor Herman said, "After this service is over, Al and his wife will be standing in front of the altar. Come on down and love on them." While I was standing on the stage when they were rolling around the Lord began to speak, and I heard him say "Alaina the stage that you are standing on being humiliated and embarrassed on will be the same stage that I will publicly raise you and your family back on....publicly." I did not quite understand the entire meaning at that time.

Now, although some of the leadership who were directly connected to Lady Herman and her armor-bearers did not like me, the members of *The Church* did. The line was wrapped around the sanctuary twice. Some of the people were waiting to give us encouraging words, and some were waiting to be nosey in order to continue the rumors that had already surfaced. Al was a basket case, but not me. I stood there for the next fifty minutes while they loved on us, and I loved on them right back. Some tried to pray for me, and I prayed for them right back. Pastor Herman had some of his elders and their wives around us to control the crowd and to console some of the members because some were very devastated and distraught.

At the end, when the crowd had dispersed, the wife of one of Lady Herman's cousins looked at me as if she was trying to come over to console me. I was trying to figure out why, because there were no tears and there was nothing for her to console. I was actually doing better than some of the people who were in attendance. She was a counselor and working on her doctorate. I am sure she was trying to analyze me, but I knew she did not like me at all.

She approached me and asked, "Sister Carpenter, can I pray for you?"

I looked her in her face, and said, "Only if I can pray for you first."

She looked at me as if to say, *This B#@%*, and I thought the same thing about her.

She said, "You are so strong."

I turned around, looked at my husband, and said, "Let's go!"

I left her standing there at the altar while I was hugging everyone else around her. I knew at that moment that I would never return to this church again. As we drove home, it was very quiet. When we arrived, the phone rang. It was Pastor Herman, but Al did not answer.

When we finally settled in to lie down, I said, "Al, you should call him back and see what he wants."

Al called Pastor Herman back and held the phone so that I can hear what was said.

Pastor Herman said, "Man, I'm still at *The Church* in my office. My wife's cousin said she tried to pray for Alaina, and she said only if she could pray for her. See, that's what I'm talking about, man. Your wife is so damn stuck up. People are trying to show her some love, and she responds like that."

For the first time since we have been in this ministry, Al stood up for me.

He said, "This is not the time for this, but since you called, my wife is not stuck up, nor does or has she ever thought she was better than anyone. You know your wife's cousin does not like my wife. The question should be why would she even want to pray for her, and why would my wife allow her to?"

I could not believe that Pastor Herman had called us for this nonsense. Nor could I believe that Al had finally stood up for me to him. The next day, I could not wait to call Bishop's wife and tell her what had happened, from the stage, to the phone tree, and to the crazy conversation that Al had with Herman. She could not believe it.

While we were talking, she said, "I hear Bishop. He's pulling into the garage." *Really?* I thought

I asked, "Can I speak to him?"

She said, "Ok."

She walked to the door while still talking to me. I could hear him going off on someone. We both asked each other who he was talking to? All I could hear was Bishop yelling. I could hear him asking whoever he was talking to, "Why are you so obsessed with her?"

She said, "Let me call you back." And hung up the phone before I could reply "Ok"

Around twenty minutes later, my phone rang.

I answered, "Hello."

It was Bishop on the other end.

Through his raspy voice, Bishop said, "Alaina, I am going to ask you this question one time."

As he was talking, I was asking myself, *"What is wrong?"*

He sounded serious, so I said, "Ok."

"Has Herman ever tried to hit on you?" he asked.

"What?" I yelled.

"Has Herman ever tried to make a pass at you?" he asked again.

"Oh my God, no sir!" I answered. "Bishop, why would you ask me something like that?"

He explained that he had been on the phone for about thirty minutes with Herman trying to figure out what to do with Al.

Bishop said, "All Herman could talk about was you. Now you know I couldn't take it, Alaina. I told him, 'Herman, your executive pastor is strung out on crack, and he may have one of your members pregnant, and all you can talk about is his wife!' I asked him why you are so obsessed with Alaina."

I was very quiet while he was talking.

He asked, "Are you there?"

"Yes, sir, I'm just speechless."

"Well, has he?" he asked.

"Bishop, I have been here for three and half years, and I have done his make-up for two years. I have been in his office alone several times.

He has never tried to hit on me. He doesn't even like me. He would ask me stupid stuff like, "Why are you so fly? Why do you dress so nice? Where do you shop? How come you won't help my wife look like a first lady? You know where Bishop's wife shops; help my wife." I thought that he was just immature and unlearned. I never took those comments to heart. I figured he just didn't know any better. He was a joke to me. Bishop, that is so gross and disgusting!"

"You are so naïve," he said.

"Now I will say this: I felt like he wanted to conquer me. That's the best way I can describe it, Bishop. He wanted me to bow down and serve him like those other weak people around him. He wants to be you in my life, Bishop, and that's not happening!"

Bishop said, "Ok, I will never ask you that again."

"Thank you!" I replied.

His wife said, "Wow, Alaina, I had no idea you were going through all of this."

I interrupted her and said, "That is just a tip of some of the things I endured."

His wife said, "I can see why she had a problem with you. It was not so much about you, but it was because of him. That is pretty low down."

"You have no idea!" I replied. "I have never talked about this to anyone but Al. You know how 'first ladies' sit on the first or second row of the church?"

"Yes," they both replied.

"Well, Lady Herman didn't. She sat on last seat of the first row against the wall, not the aisle seat that would be closest to where Pastor Herman would minister from and that everyone would know that she was the 'first lady.' There were around eighteen chairs on each row. She sat in the eighteenth chair, which was off in the cut to where no one could see her. There were eight to ten rows in front of the row she sat, on both sides of the altar, facing each other. This is where the ministers and their wives along with the altar workers sat. On the front row of this section is where Pastor Herman and his armor-bearer would sit. The Sunday after the announcement of Al becoming the executive pastor, when we entered the sanctuary, I noticed there were three seats on the front row. I assumed that was for Pastor Herman, Lady Herman, and Al. I went and sat behind Al. When Pastor Herman came out, his armor-bearer sat next to me, and Herman sat in the first seat, leaving the middle chair open. I looked back, and Lady Herman was still sitting in her usual seat off in the cut. Pastor Herman looked back at me and said, 'Why are you sitting back there?'

"I had the most confused look on my face. I responded, 'I thought that seat was for your wife.'

"He then looked at me with an even more confused look and said, 'Naw, this seat is for you. Come up here.'

"I looked at Al like what is going on. I waited for a few seconds before moving. I finally moved my seat. It was so uncomfortable. There I sat on the front row between Pastor Herman and my husband while his wife sat behind me off in the cut. This was not a good look. For the next three months or so, the seating arrangements didn't change. I would beg Al, 'Please tell Pastor Herman to move his wife up on the front row.' This is not fair to her or me. I am not the First Lady!

"Al would say, 'Bae, I have, and his response would be she is fine where she is.'" I don't know why he doesn't want his wife on the front row.

Bishop's wife said, "Alaina, you have to be making this up."

I responded, "I wish I was. Can you imagine what I went through at that church?" Just because of that alone.

"Did he ever move her up?" she asked.

"Yes, after a few months or so. I believe the move was made only because we made a big fuss about it." Al would continue to try to show Pastor Herman how bad this looked and how uncomfortable it made me.

"I am so sorry that you had to endure this."

I said, "I know, and even though I did not think it was my responsibility, I still tried to help step her game up."

"I agree that she was not where she needs to be in her appearance as a first lady. What do you mean you tried to help her?" she asked.

I replied, "Ok, I will give one example. I noticed every time I would see her she would have an orange tint on her face and black eyeliner around her lips."

She laughed, and asked, "Orange?"

"Yep, orange, and don't forget the liner. I think she was wearing Fashion Fair, and it just was not the right color for her skin tone.

"One Sunday after service, I asked NeNe, who sang on the praise team and also worked for MAC Cosmetics, if she would do me a big favor. She said sure. I explained to her that I did not want her to discuss this with anyone. She replied ok.

"When you go to work, can you please get Lady Herman everything she needs from foundation, powder, blush, eye shadow, lipstick, etc.?"

NeNe looked at me and said, "Oh my God, I've wanted to do this a while ago. I just didn't know how to approach her, and I did not want to offend her. I noticed that she is always orange."

I said, "I know, but I'm just trying to help."

NeNe asked, "Are you going to do her hair too?"

"Girl, one thing at a time. Let's get this done first, and besides she loves her current stylist and how she does her hair."

"I explained that I didn't care how much it cost. I would pay for it. So Wednesday before Bible study, NeNe brought me two bags of stuff that cost over a hundred and twenty-five dollars and that was after her sixty percent discount. I went into Lady Herman's office before she got there and laid it all out on her desk.

"When Lady Herman came into the sanctuary for worship, she sat next to me and whispered in my ear, 'Sister Carpenter, I know nobody but you did that in my office.'

"I smiled at her, and said, 'Yes, I'm guilty.'

"She was visibly excited and asked, 'Why did you do that? That was so nice of you.'

"Why did she have to ask me this?

"I smiled back and said, 'Well, you have been a bit orange.'

"'Orange?' she asked with this weird giggle she would do. 'Oh my God, I thought I was cute.'

"I laughed back and said, 'You are cute just with a hint of orange.'

"I was so happy that she made light of it."

"Then she said, 'Thank you.' We hugged."

I suggested to Bishop's wife that she should have a class to help pastors' wives look like first ladies and how they should conduct themselves, and she politely declined.

After I got off the phone, I thought about a conversation that Mona and I had about a year and a half prior. She'd told me that her other friend, Tee, used to date Pastor Herman.

I said, "No way! How did he get with her?"

Now I knew Tee very well, and for years, people said that we looked just alike. I did not know that she had dated Pastor Herman. Tee was sharp. She always had her stuff together. Her hair was always on point, and she could dress her butt off. Tee came from a well-to-do family, and she had graduated from college. Herman was not her type at all. I only knew of one of Tee's exes. They dated forever, and he was just as fly as Tee. He was well known in the city. He was a hustler, and quite the opposite of Herman.

Now I did not know Pastor Herman before coming to the church, but when one of my clients came to get her hair done, she explained how she was visiting the church the day Pastor Herman introduced Al as the executive pastor. She saw us both up there. She said how proud she was of us. In the conversation, she explained how she grew up with Pastor Herman and that they had graduated from high school together.

"Boy, has he come a long way," she stated.

"What do you mean?" I asked.

"Girl, he was a lame in school, and he could not dress at all. He was a cornball. He wanted to be so popular in school. He tried sports, but he was not good at all. Nobody would date him."

She had several funny stories of him trying to get a girlfriend. One day she and her and her friends played a joke on him. They told him that they were having a house party after school and that if he came, not only was he going to get a girlfriend, but also he was also going to get laid. Their whole class knew about the prank. Sure enough, around four o'clock, he knocked at the door.

She opened the door and asked, "Yes, what are you doing here?"

He said, "I'm here for the party."

I could not let her finish the story because I was cracking up laughing.

She said, "Girl, we laughed at him the whole year. It was the joke of the school. Everyone knew, including the principal and teachers."

"You all were wrong for that," I said, but it was funny.

While we were at Bible study one night, Pastor Herman kept looking toward our section.

I asked, "Mona, why does he keep looking over here?"

Mona laughed and said, "Girl, he probably thinks you're Tee."

I said, "You're sick."

"No, for real, he really liked her. You know y'all look just alike."

"I can't even imagine Tee going out with him," I said.

"They did," she replied.

"Girl, Lady Herman could not stand Tee."

Tee said she would go to church with him when he was a youth pastor at another church. She would get dressed up on purpose, and Lady Herman would be so mad.

I said, "Tee is a fool."

We both laughed. Pastor Herman was so irritated with us for talking and laughing while he was teaching. The more he looked at us, the funnier it got. We knew better than to be laughing in church, but sometimes that was when it was the funniest. At one point, Lady Herman turned around because I guess she could hear us or she was trying to see why her husband kept looking over there. When she looked at me, the tears were rolling down my face because I could not stop laughing. Lady Herman even giggled because I was laughing so hard. Mona would not stop.

I asked, "Can you imagine Tee being a first lady?"

We were cracking up in church. We didn't hear anything Pastor Herman said that night.

CHAPTER 7

Talk of the Town

Thursday was horrible. I was up pretty much all night. When I finally dozed off, it was time to get up. I woke up with a bad headache. As I got ready for work, I was nervous. I got my girls ready for school. I was extremely quiet. I explained to them that I was not feeling well. I drove my girls to school in a daze. It was such a dreary day. It was raining outside, and there was no sun at all. As I approached my job, I didn't know what to expect. While managing twenty-plus women, anything was liable to happen. As I walked in, it appeared that everyone was talking. I hid myself in my office. I only came out if I had to.

It was all over Cleveland. It was in the streets, the salons, the barbershops, and other churches. The story had grown so big and had so much added on to it that I didn't even recognize it anymore. The peace and strength that I had on Wednesday night was depleted. I became weak and feeble all over again. I still had not eaten a full meal in over three weeks. Mona would bring me fresh fruit, and she had introduced me to Bolt House Smoothies, which was how I was getting my nutrients. I stayed as long as I could before I had to leave. I took a half day's worth of sick time. I went home, took four Advil, and went to sleep.

By Friday, I had a migraine out of this world. Al had gone on one of his binges again, and I did not care this time. I was getting sick, and my health was not right. I got to work on Friday, and I told the receptionist no phone calls today because I still was not feeling well. I was in my office with the lights off, and my head plastered to the desk. I was in so much pain.

Mona called, and I agreed to take the call.

Mona said, "If you're not better by the time you get off, I'm taking you to the emergency room. This is not healthy, and I'm concerned about you."

I said, "You're concerned about me? Girl, you're in labor and having contractions, and you don't even know it. You're about to have this baby, so if anyone is going to be in the hospital, it is going to be you!"

As I continued to lie there, I could feel the tears begin to flow. I didn't know I had any tears left. The phone rang, and I thought, *I said no phone calls*. With my head still plastered to the desk, I picked up the phone and laid it on top of my right ear.

I said, "Yes."

The receptionist said, "I know you said no phone calls, but this sounded important. It's Pastor Herman, and he said that he needs to speak with you."

I said, "Ok, put him through."

I was still in the same position with my head on the desk and the phone resting on my right ear. I could not even hold the phone because my head was pounding so badly. My voice was so weak.

I quietly said, "Yes."

He said, "Sister Carpenter, I know you're going through a really rough time right now, but I heard you were back at your old church with Bishop?"

You have got to be kidding me.

I responded after a long pause, "Yes."

Then in his street slang Pastor Herman said, "I mean, Bishop ain't doing anything for you and Al. I pay Al X, Y, and Z. Al ain't never made this kind of money before. I'm sending y'all to counseling and putting a severance package together for y'all. Bishop ain't doing nothing but running his mouth. Where is your loyalty?"

He was going on and on, and I would not respond.

Then he asked, "How come I can't be yo' daddy?"

He loved for people to refer to him as "Daddy."

I was shocked and asked, "What? Do you mean spiritual father?" My voice was very, very, weak, cracking, and raspy. "Can you hear me?"

He said, "Yeah, yeah, I hear you."

I sat up, with the room spinning around fast and my head pounding.

I told him, "I am going to tell you why you will never be my spiritual father!"

When Pastor Herman would preach, he loved to give examples so he could make things clear. He would say, "Let me *Hermanize* it," Ebonics-style. I gave him an example that would hit very close to home so he would clearly understand what I meant. I did this without any reservations because I would never have this conversation again.

"You know how when you married Lady Herman and she had already two kids, Chenell and Dietrick?"

He replied, "Yeah, yeah."

I said, "I don't care how many Coach bags you buy Chenell and how many Timberland boots you buy Dietrick, those two will never be your children. Those are Red's kids! That is Red's blood running through their veins! Al and I came to you equipped. We were a blessing to this ministry. We brought our training from our previous church to help you with your vision here. You didn't birth us into anything. That is why you will never be my spiritual father. At best you are my *little brother* in the spirit."

He said, "Oh, oh, oh, you don't have to ever worry about me calling you again."

Then he hung the phone up. I slammed the phone down because I could not believe this man would call me with some BS like this. I was pissed off at this point. The room was still spinning, and my head was still pounding. Finally, I laid my head back down on the desk. I closed my eyes.

Ring! Ring! Ring!

It's was the phone again. I was thinking, *"This better be God on the other end of this phone."*

I snatched the phone up, and yelled, "Hello!"

"Sister Carpenter, it's Lady Herman. My husband just called me and said you were talking about my kids. My husband loves my kids. Can you please keep their names out of your mouth?"

I did not let her get the word "mouth" out good.

I said, "I didn't call your husband; he called me. He was harassing me. I'm going through the worst time of my life right now. I don't give a crap about you, your husband, or your damn kids! I'm telling you like I told him to leave me the hell alone!"

"Ok, Sister Carpenter, he won't call you anymore."

Once she said that, I hung up the phone.

CHAPTER 8

The Counseling Session

Wednesday approached, and it was payday. I was looking for the check, so I called *The Church* as I was instructed. I was transferred to Pastor Herman's secretary. I was told that there was no check for Brother Al this week.

"Did you guys forget it? Is it just not cut yet? When should we receive our severance package? Are you guys still paying for counseling?" I had a lot of these types of questions running through my mind.

"Sister Carpenter, you can call the House of Our Father. The sessions have already been paid for. We will get back to you concerning the check and the severance package," the secretary stated.

I hung up and called the House of Our Father. We were able to get an appointment for the next day. I called Al to let him know that we didn't get a check.

He asked, "Really? Oh he is tripping. Don't ask him for nothing else. I got us in this mess, and I am going to get us out. I'm looking for a job now. I have a few interviews set up. We will go to counseling, and that's it." Al was very upset about the check. I'm not sure if he and Pastor Herman had words but he was adamant about me not calling the church back.

The next day came, and I did not want to go to the counseling session, although we needed it. At this point, I didn't trust anyone. The counselor would be Bishop Tim, who was Pastor Herman's pastor, which made it very uncomfortable for me. Being in ministry for over twenty plus years, I had seen many games being played through pastors, bishops, leaders and their wives. You go in and share personal and confidential information, and then the next thing you know, it is being told over the pulpit or discussed with their families and other leaders. That is why I did not want to speak with Bishop Tim. Although I had never heard anything negative about him, I still did not trust it. I was extremely vulnerable and fearful, but knowing that we needed help, we made a decision to go ahead and go. We were definitely not going to be counseled by Pastor Herman.

We pulled up to the House of Our Father and went inside where we were greeted by the receptionist. As we checked in and were about to take our seats, Bishop Tim's wife came in and greeted us. She embraced me with the warmest hug. I almost wished she were doing our counseling session and not her husband.

She said, "Follow me. I'm going to take you to the bishop's office."

He opened the door, and he was dressed in full clergy.

"Hey there, y'all. How are you doing? Come on in and have a seat," he stated.

He was trying to make light of the situation, but it was too late. We were both very heavy-hearted and broken.

"How is everything going?" he asked with a smile.

Al said, "It could be better."

I didn't say anything, but if looks could kill, mine certainly would have.

"Sister Carpenter, are you ok today?" he asked.

"No, I am not! I don't want to be here," I told him as he looked at me like I was crazy. "Bishop Tim I don't mean no disrespect but I don't trust you. I know the games that you leaders play--"

He cut me off and said, "Wait a minute. Wait a minute. What are you talking about?"

"I know that you probably want me to sit here and pour my heart out, and as soon as I get out the door, you're going to call Pastor Herman and tell him everything," I said.

He tried to reassure me and said, "Sister Carpenter, I am a licensed counselor, and I am mandated by the state of Ohio to the strictest of confidentiality. I would never go back and do that. I will let you know that anything as far as ministry I will share with Pastor Herman only because of the level of leadership that you guys are in. I promise you I will not share any of your personal information with him."

With him giving me his word, I said, "Ok."

I began to share with him that although Al made horrible choices, which lead us here, he did not get us here alone. With Pastor Herman's abusive, enticing, manipulating, and demanding style of leadership as well as his insecurities, he had a way of encouraging his leaders to believe that they were obligated to serve him as if he was their god. Many leaders had given up good jobs to serve him and *"The Church."*

Bishop Tim reiterated exactly what I'd said to make sure he'd understood me correctly. Although he listened to me, he did not look surprised.

"Bishop, I know that we are here to deal with the affair, but I can't even start there because it has been so much that has happened to us that lead us to this point."

"Ok, Sister Carpenter, where would you like to start?" he asked.

"They are so insecure," I said.

"Who are they?" Bishop Tim asked.

"Pastor Herman and his wife," I said.

"Give me an example of his insecurity?" he asked.

I'm not sure if he knew what he was asking of me, because I had plenty of examples. The question should have been if we had enough time in this session to list them all.

"Ok," I replied. "Pastor Herman finally decided that he would take a vacation after pastoring for two years, and he left Al in charge. Al was supposed to preach both services on Sunday and teach at Wednesday night Bible study. Al preached his butt off, and *The Church* didn't miss a beat. It was just as if Pastor Herman was there. Over sixty souls came to Christ and joined *The Church*. Al was so excited that everything went well and that he could be trusted in Pastor Herman's absence. Everyone was saying how well Pastor Al did. They were making comments like, "Pastor Herman can stay another week" and "We really enjoyed Pastor Al." He could not wait until Pastor Herman returned so he could let him know. Pastor Herman returned and called a meeting with Al. We later found out that one of his 'Secret Service' boys (armor-bearers) had called him while he was on vacation to inform him how well Pastor Al did and what the people were saying.

"Now, Bishop Tim, you would think that he would be happy, right? He went off on Al. He told him, 'Nigga, don't you ever preach like that in my church! This is my church, and I'm the pastor.'

After Pastor Herman had that meeting, he didn't allow Al to preach again for almost a year. He preferred people who could not preach a lick preach before he would call on Al. He liked to hear the people complain and say they were not coming to church if he was not going to be preaching.

"Bishop Tim, one day as we were leaving church, and Al and I were holding hands walking to the car, Al opened my door and I got in. Pastor Herman was getting in his car which was parked next to ours. He asked, 'Hey, Al, why does your family have to be so perfect? You and Alaina always seem so happy, your kids are so smart, and they always look good. Nobody's family is that perfect.'

Bishop, I could not believe he would say that. We never said that our marriage was perfect. That is what he thought. I told Al when we pulled off that he was so jealous of you. Al disagreed, although he felt weird about the comment.

One day after service he asked, Al how do you worship God like you do and have tears rolling down your face in all three services. He said, 'I know when people are gaming, but you are so sincere. I may feel his presence in one or two services, but not like you do. What is that?'

Al explained it was spending quality time with God privately in daily devotions. He said, 'I start my day off around five thirty or six every morning for the last fifteen years. It comes from a relationship.' The very next Sunday, this man gets up and preaches about what Al had just shared with him. Bishop Tim, how do you preach about something that you have not experienced?"

Bishop Tim was trying to keep a straight face.

"Bishop, the people loved us. Al was the first point of contact for everything concerning *The Church*, so the people got to know Al on a personal level. He is gifted and anointed, and he never put himself above them. He was able to relate to them. Al had his bachelor's degree and was now working on his master's degree. Because of Al's unbearable schedule, he had to drop out of the master's program to give his attention to the various roles at the church. Pastor Herman told Al that was a good decision; he needed him to be focused on the things for the church.

"Meanwhile, Herman continued to take accelerated courses out of the city to get his degree so he could pass Al. He would say, 'You can't be the only one with a degree.' He had only had a high school diploma at this time. Al had been trained by Bishop for years. He had everything going for him. He was not just loved in the church; he was loved in the streets. Al was very popular in Cleveland because of basketball. To know him was to love him. Everything Herman ever wanted to be, from being popular in school, to the basketball court, and to the pulpit, Al already was. He always wanted his leaders to be beneath him, which takes me back to the day that he had all the current pastors in *The Church* on the stage. He announced to them and the congregation that he would be the only one in the church who would utilize the title of pastor. Every other pastor would be stripped of their titles and would be named as elders going forward.

"Bishop, you were there that night. How do you reordain someone who has already been ordained? Al came there as an ordained elder. I will tell you how. It is to make yourself feel superior.

"He was so narcissistic. The sad part was that Al was happy with just helping him in the ministry. He never wanted to be in the front. I won't go back completely, but you remember Leonard Homes, the CFO that came from Chicago? He brought his wife, two daughters, and his young assistant to Cleveland. I had Bishop call you because we knew he was a crook and you would be able to talk to Pastor Herman and protect the ten thousand members of *The Church*. I met Leonard at my old church. Bishop and I knew he was responsible for two pastors being in prison because of his fraudulent practices. I tried to warn Pastor Herman about him, but he had already taken the bait. Leonard promised him that he would never go back to the projects or be broke again and he would get him a bigger house, his dream cars, and so on. Those were things that Al could not deliver. Leonard came through just like he said. All the while he was sleeping with his assistant and every other woman in the church. It killed Pastor Herman that he had to let Leonard go. He tried to justify why Leonard should stay. Even though he was caught in a moral sin ten times over from what Al had done? He didn't make Leonard Homes and his wife go on the stage. He made every excuse as to why he was not going to publicly discipline him. Pastor Herman protected Leonard at all costs. After Leonard was released from the church, the rumor was that they went into business together. They did this so that Leonard could fulfill the rest of his promises that he made to Pastor Herman. He was more concerned about his gain than anything else. That's what I mean by insecure.

"Bishop Tim, I have a question for you."

"Ok," he replied.

"Why would a pastor who is supposed to be a man of God idolize *Scarface*? It is his favorite movie."

"What's wrong with that?" Bishop Tim asked.

"I like the movie too, but just hear me out. For his thirty-eighth birthday party that was held at the church, the theme was Scarface. They had masks for all the guests, which was the face of Tony Montana. You have been to his house, and I know you saw that his whole basement has life-sized posters of Tony Montana throughout. He talks about the movie with such admiration. It's like he wants to run the church like Tony ran his dynasty. This movie is a tale of ferocious greed, corruption, and power, the darker side of the fabled American dream.

"There are definitely some similarities between Pastor Herman and Tony Montana. They both came from nothing but wanted everything, regardless of who they had to step on in order to get it. Tony wanted to rule the world, and Herman wanted notoriety and power in his hometown by any means necessary. This might be ok for a gangster in a movie but not for a man of God, in my opinion."

Bishop Tim was listening to every word that I was saying. I was so full I had been holding all this in for over three years.

"I was just as vulnerable as Al, and the truth of the matter, Bishop, is that I could have had an affair as well, but I didn't. I honored my vows to my husband as well as my covenant to God. I just had a different set of standards and morals than Al. Pastor Herman had driven a wedge in our home where only Al and I existed. We lived in the same house and slept in the same bed, but his loyalty was to Herman. Al betrayed our marriage long before he ever slept with Tiffany."

"Alaina, you said that Al betrayed your marriage long before the affair. What do you mean by that?" Bishop Tim asked.

"Ok, I have never shared this story with anyone but I will share this with you to explain what I mean. Al and I have been together since I was sixteen years old, and we have never talked about any of our personal information to anyone. After I had talked to Al about his outrageous schedule, I thought I would take matters in my own hand. I called Al's secretary and made an appointment on his calendar for Tuesday at noon.

"As I got ready for my appointment with Pastor Al, I did my hair and make-up just like he liked it, I put on his favorite perfume, and I wore a nice two-piece from Victoria's Secret with a trench coat and a tall pair of thigh-high boots. When I arrived at his office, the secretary called back and said, 'Pastor Al, your next appointment has arrived. It's Sister Alaina.'

"He said, 'That sounds like my wife.' Al came out to get me, but I was already walking to his office. Al said, 'What are you doing here?'

"I said, 'Since I can't spend time with you at home, I thought I would come and see you here.' As Al closed his door, I said, 'Lock it.' His office would never be the same. Bishop that is all I'm going to say about his office. I will just leave it there.

"That was on a Tuesday. I went to Bible study the next day. When Lady Herman came out to the sanctuary, she was smiling unusually hard at me. During the service she leaned over and said, 'Sister Carpenter, I heard what you did to Pastor Al.'

I immediately turned red and said, 'What did you hear?'

She responded, "Girl, thanks for the tip. I'm going to take care of Pastor Herman tomorrow.'

I have never felt so embarrassed; I could not believe that Al had shared such personal information about me with another man. I didn't know who he was anymore and what all did he tell Herman. Did he tell him everything we did in his office? What was Herman thinking when he would see me? And what did he say to his wife to make her feel that she had to do what I did? This was very uncomfortable for me. It was like Al was brainwashed. He was not in his right mind, Al had drunk the Kool-Aid. He was gone and there was nothing that I could do.

Al sat there as I explained. Bishop Tim looked at Al, but he was not present. "Why do you say that Pastor Herman drove a wedge in your home?"

"Not only was Al's schedule an issue, but every other day he had something to say to Al about me. 'Your wife so stuck up, your wife thinks she is better than my wife, your wife didn't give the secretary your home phone number.' It was always your wife, your wife, your wife. He even went as far as to say, 'You need to get your wife in check. I pay you X, Y, and Z.' He continued to throw what he was getting paid in Al's face. Al never stood up to him, nor did he protect me. He would just say, 'Bae, we are more spiritual than they are so just ignore him. I know that you are not like that. God has us here to help this man.'"

Bishop Tim said, "Alaina, it appears that Pastor Herman is not one of your favorite people. You really don't have much respect for him do you?"

"Bishop, I lost respect for him a long time ago when he was bragging in one of our meetings about when he was the youth pastor at Lady

Herman's father's church. She and her ex-husband came in for counseling. He advised her to leave him, and when she did, not long afterwards, he married her. I'm old school, so first of all, why would a single youth pastor be counseling a married couple? To add insult to injury, he would get up in the pulpit on Sunday mornings and brag about the material things that he had at their home. He would say it was like an arcade and the kids never wanted to leave to go spend time with their real dad because he could not compete with all the gifts and gadgets. Not only do I not have respect for him. But also I don't have any respect for his wife either. When he would make those stupid announcements, she would sit back and do that dumb giggle. She did so as if it were cute instead of not allowing him to disrespect her kid's father. He was probably doing the best he could do."

I gave Bishop Tim an earful of three and a half years' worth of stuff. I had so much more to say.

Bishop Tim looked at Al, and said, "Wow, all this was going on?"

Al responded, "Yes, sir."

Bishop Tim tried to explain to me that I was raised similar to him, how he was brought up in a Pentecostal background, and that he could understand how it was difficult for me to be in a ministry that was more liberal. I explained to him that the church was not all bad. I had seen it help a lot of people, and hurt a lot as well. It was not a place that my family should have been at. I felt as if I had received my PhD and returned to preschool. It is good for people who are new to Christ. I felt like I was dying spiritually. I needed more. The environment was hostile, and it was not conducive for growth for me. If I had just been a member and not in leadership, it may have been different.

Although our session was supposed to be forty-five minutes, it went over, and I believe I vented the entire time. I was not giving Al room to say a word because he had already done enough damage. Al had failed me and our kids. He was not just my husband or just their dad; he was our pastor as well. We ended our session, and our homework assignment was to read the book *Torn Asunder*.

We made an appointment for the next session for the following week and then took our book and left. We sat in the car for approximately ten minutes and talked about what had just happened. We both cried. Al was very apologetic. He was not only apologizing for the affair, but also for bringing his family into this ministry. We pulled out the parking lot to get on 77 North to head home. We had barely made it past two exits when the phone rang. It was Pastor Herman, and Al answered. I immediately heard Pastor Herman yelling through the other end of the phone.

Pastor Herman asked, "Al, what's this I hear that your wife was in the office talking about me like I'm a dog?"

I said, "Do you see what I mean, Al? It happened just that quickly. We haven't been gone twenty minutes, and he already knows what we talked about in our session."

After Al and I talked, we both agreed that we did not think that Bishop Tim had totally reneged on what he promised me in that office. I believed in my heart that once he saw how sincere I was in what I was saying, he felt the need to call and deal with Pastor Herman on a ministerial level as his leader. I knew that Pastor Herman was immature and shallow in his thinking and probably took what Bishop Tim had said to him and twisted it how he saw fit. After all, he was a man who thought he was always right and could not handle being chastised or criticized. We could not handle the idea of any more betrayal, so we never returned for another session. Still not receiving any help or counseling. I felt like the women with the issue of blood.... Instead of my situation getting better it grew worse.

CHAPTER 9

No Payment

A week had passed, and I still had not received Al's last check. I called *The Church*, and Pastor Herman would not have a conversation with me. I spoke with the director of finance, and she informed me that not only would Al not be receiving his last check, but also he would not be receiving his severance package. I was very confused.

I started asking questions. "What do you mean? Is the budget short? Does he need to wait another week? What do you mean?" Was Pastor Herman doing this because I would not let him control me or because I was vocal in how I felt?

She said, "Sister Carpenter, I'm sorry."

I was shocked because, as I said earlier, this was not the first scandal that this church had seen. The administrator before Al committed an illegal offense, a crime. He should have been put in jail for a very long time, but Pastor Herman and his people decided not to report it to the authorities. They took matters into their own hands and went the spiritual route, not the legal route. Not only did they do that, but also they paid him a ten-thousand-dollar severance package and gave him counseling.

So why would I not think that Al would get paid? Yes, he had committed a sin and backslid as a pastor, but it wasn't illegal it was unethical.

One thing for sure is that he certainly never molested or raped anyone, and he sure as heck didn't get paid off for it. That's all I've got to say about that! I was sure that we were denied our last check because I would not conform nor would I be controlled. Al was also upset, but he was still struggling with crack. He could not deal with anything he was only concerned about he would fund his next high.

CHAPTER 10

The Job Offer

So, what are we going to do? We were both embarrassed. Al could not live with the guilt of facing the people here in Cleveland. I was scared to go outside. I do not want my kids hearing anything in the streets. Al had started to look for a job because they had taken away sixty-five thousand dollars of our income. He looked for a job, but it was to no avail. I was making enough to support us, but we needed that severance package to reestablish ourselves. Now we had to go back to the drawing board. Our good friend Robbin Taylor had relocated to Atlanta, Georgia, and she was one of the managers at the Centers for Disease Control.

Al had worked for her in Cleveland when she was managing TRW Inc. She heard what happened and called Al to verify what she heard; he confirmed everything. She asked Al what his plan was, and he said he didn't have an idea, but he was looking for a job. Robbin was always resourceful when it came to finding jobs and employing people. She told Al she had a position that was available in Atlanta, but he would have to start on the following Monday. This was on Tuesday when Al had spoken with her. Our daughter Lauren was graduating from Roxboro Middle School on Thursday. Pastor Herman had planted in Al's head that nobody would ever pay him the kind of money he was paying him. I always wondered why he would keep saying that. Now don't get me wrong: I was grateful for the salary my husband was making, but sixty-five thousand dollars a year? He made it seem like he was paying him six figures. The position at

CDC started him off with eighty-five thousand a year. My, my, my, was Pastor Herman wrong.

As Al began to sell me on this move to Atlanta, he explained the starting salary not only was a pay increase but also there was room for growth.

Wow, I thought. I figured this would get us out of Cleveland and give us a break from all this drama. It would also allow us to protect our kids at the same time. I was already a manager at JCPenney, so I told him to let me see if my job would transfer me. Al was not going to wait to see if my job would move me. He had to let Robbin know the next day. Robbin called me that night to see how the girls and I were. She wanted to assure me that this was all legit and that she would help us. She was like our big sister, and we trusted her.

He went ahead and accepted the job with Robbin. After our daughter's graduation, he planned to drive his truck down to Atlanta, and that is just what he did. I was scared to death because I was thinking how we could up and go to another city with no preparation, no house, and no knowledge of the school system. I would have to uproot our children to follow a drug-addicted husband. I rationalized everything. If my job said I could do a transfer and keep my same salary, then it must be God!

I went to work and met with my manager. They explained to me that there was a job opening at Buford Mall in Georgia. Since I had done such a great job at the JCPenney here at Richmond Mall, they were eager to have me and hoped I could do the same thing there. So now we are once again back at the six-figure mark. By this time, I still had not dealt with the affair, the abuse of the ministry, the public humiliation on the stage, the possibility of my husband having a baby because I was dealing with his drug addiction. Now I have to pack up and move to a new city with two kids, ages nine and thirteen. They had no idea about what was even going on. I also have to tell my family that we were leaving. After Lauren's graduation, we went out to dinner and told the kids the news of relocating to Atlanta. (I did not know how they would react. The day after Al had spoken to Robbin about the job I played around with the idea of us relocating with the girls to see their reaction. It appeared that they would like to move and have their daddy back and do anything to get away from "The Church." They were so excited and were ready to go home and pack.

Al would be leaving for Atlanta on Saturday, and I would be moving in two weeks once my job completed my transfer. Now I had to break the news to my family. How was I going to tell my mom who I hadn't told anything by this time, we were leaving?

My mother asked, "Alaina, what is going on? I have heard so many uncertain stories, but I want to hear it from you. Is Al all right?"

I said, "Ma, Al is fine. You know he lost his position at "The Church." He didn't handle it right, but he's good now. He got a good job offer in Atlanta making eighty-five thousand dollars a year, and my job is going to transfer me to Atlanta also."

"Atlanta? What do you mean Atlanta? What about my grandkids? Are you taking my grandkids away from me? Is Al making you do this? I will kill him! Alaina, you do not have to go. Let Al go, and you and the kids can stay here. You can move in with me. Let him go down there first and get settled. Then he can send for you once he has himself together."

"No, Ma, I have to go with my husband. He is leaving Saturday and starting his new job on Monday. I am leaving in two weeks."

She lost it. She fell out and burst into tears. Alaina, I don't like this one bit!

She said, "Before you leave I need to look him in his face and speak directly to him."

I answered, "Yes, ma'am."

When I left my mother's home, I called my sister to have her meet me at my house so I could tell her the news as well. I knew that this would be difficult because I love my sister to pieces. We were very close. As Dee Dee came into the house, she walked into my bedroom, and we sat on my bed. I did not open my mouth. Without me saying a word, we both broke down and cried. I knew my mother had already gotten to her and my brother. As I looked at her I said I know you know I'm moving to Atlanta... she nodded yes with tears rolling down her face. It killed me to see her cry, as it did her watching me in pain.

"Dee Dee, you know I am not crazy, and you know if I felt this was not right I would not be going. I promise you if this does not work out, then I am coming back home on the first thing smoking," I told her as we hugged and cried.

It seemed as if hours had passed. Indeed, this was one of the most challenging things I had to do.

After breaking the news to my family, I needed to talk this through with someone I trusted, and that was not connected to any of this. So I called Pastor Gwendolyn McCurry. She had done our premarital counseling, and we had worked with her in the ministry for years. Pastor McCurry had been counseling and prayed for us since I had found out everything. I didn't trust anyone as I believed her. She was a pastor's Pastor. She was trustworthy.

I went to her home, and she prayed for my children and me. She thought this was a good move. It would allow the fire to die down because she did not believe Al would survive in Cleveland. My conversation with her made my decision to go more logical because I trusted her. As I was leaving out the door, she began to prophesy over my girls and said she saw them on a stage and their names in lights and that they would be known nationally. She told me my children would go through the fire, but they would not get burned. This time with her made me feel like I could make it, and as crazy as all this was, I was encouraged.

CHAPTER 11

Atlanta – A New Beginning

Fast forward to two weeks later, and it was now time for the girls and me to leave for Atlanta. Al flew in to help me drive my car back down. I had not seen Al for two weeks, but we talked every day. He assured me that everything was okay over there. He told me he had not gotten high in a very long time. He also said he had been to work on time every day, and Robbin confirmed it. He told me how much I was going to love Atlanta. Al explained that he had gone to look at a new house in a beautiful housing development, and he got the approval without my income. He sold me on a fresh start away from all the noise, and I believed him. I needed my family to work so bad because we had no riches, and I was a product of a broken home; I didn't ever want my kids to go through that, so whatever I had to do was what I did.

We picked Al up from the airport, and as we did, I was sizing him up. I was looking at him, smelling him, and looking into his eyes to see if they were red from drinking and getting high. I needed to make sure we were good at making this seven-hundred-mile journey. He looked perfect. He had new clothes and a fresh haircut. He smelled good, looked well, and he was saying all the right things. He even had pictures of the new house that he had picked for us. After we left the airport, we went home, and he spent some time with the girls. We ate dinner and showed the girls our new house; and he explained our home was not going to be ready for a week and we would be staying in an Extend Stay hotel until we moved in. Al promised them he was not getting back into the ministry, and he apologized for not being home and for putting the ministry before the family. As we finished dinner the girls were so happy to hear that, and it made moving to Atlanta the right choice. It appeared our family would be together again.

I went back to packing because we were leaving in the morning. Al said, "Let me go make a run to go see my parents and get the car gassed up. I'll be back once I am done in like an hour or so."

He left the house at around seven that evening. I lost track of time because I was packing. Nine o'clock rolled around, and there was no Al. Then eleven o'clock turned around, and there was no Al. Then one a.m. and four a.m. turned, and there was still no Al. I called his cell phone, and it was going straight to his voicemail. Now it was six a.m., and there was still no Al. I had been up all night, crying and praying. Now I had a decision to make. Do I stay here, or do I go with him? The kids woke up, and they were so excited about their new life and their new house.

They started to ask where Daddy was. I told them he would be back because he went to get gas. I suggested that we just keep packing. Around 9:45 that morning in comes Al, and he was sweating profusely. I sent the girls downstairs to watch a movie. Then I physically attacked Al. I hit him with everything I had. I choked him. Oh! This can't be happening to me, He deceived me big time, he never left his 'high' life. He just let me do it while promising me that it would never happen again. I told him I wasn't going. The kids came upstairs and asked if I was ready to go. I looked in their eyes, and I didn't want to disappoint them, I was so scared and confused. I decided to leave because I thought it would be best for my family. I didn't know what else to do. We left around eleven o'clock in the morning with neither of us having any sleep. I threw on my Donnie McClurkin and Kirk Franklin CDs, and I cried all the way for over seven hundred miles. The song that got me through was Kirk Franklin and Marvin Winan's "Brokenhearted."

"Come ye brokenhearted, come ye weary soul,

There is healing water that can make you whole

ALAINA HOLLOWAY-CARPENTER

That can make you whole

Come bring tears of sorrow, come bring years of pain,

There is healing water that can make you whole

That can make you whole

And it flows through the veins of Jesus

My savior, my healer, and redeemer a lover so true

It has the power to heal all our sin-sick diseases

So come to the throne your healing is here that can that can that can make you whole.

Your healing is here, forgiveness is here, salvation is here, acceptance is here, deliverance is here, His Presence is here, his mercy is here, his power is here, joy is here Grace is here, love is here that can make you whole. That can make you whole.

I kept wondering if this song was indeed true. Although I knew God was able to do this, I was just so broken, and everything seemed so far away.

CHAPTER 12

A Whirlwind

It was July fourth weekend, and we had finally made it to Atlanta and our new beginning. Our house was not ready, so we had to stay at an extended-stay hotel for a week and a half. After that, we were finally moved into our new home, Al had picked out. It was brand new and beautiful, just like he'd said. I was running around trying to get everything situated. I had to go shopping to get items to make the girls' bedrooms and bathrooms perfect for them. Then there was registering them for their new schools, getting their shot records, and getting them everything that was required to start a new school. I also had to go on a tour of the school, meet the teachers, discuss class schedules, find bus routes, and get Allyson signed up to play basketball. Everything was on a fast pace, but it was all worth it for our new beginning.

Then there was getting myself prepared for my new job. This salon was a failing salon, and they were expecting so much out of me. They needed me to take nine-operator salon to a twenty-five-operator salon functioning at full capacity. They had a goal for me to increase sales and duplicate what I'd done in Cleveland at the Richmond Mall, which was almost impossible. I had to visit beauty schools to recruit stylists. I was driving around a city I knew nothing about. I was consistently getting lost and stuck in traffic, and I was still not meeting any of my goals.

The pressure of the salon and home, while still dealing with a drug-addicted husband, was too much. I needed relief! I thought I've got to find me a church home. I was in Atlanta, which could be considered Bible Central, and I had so many churches to choose from. Because of my relationship with Bishop, I knew so many of the pastors. I went to the largest church in Atlanta. I made an appointment, because not only did I need a church home, but also, we needed counseling. We still had not dealt with any of our issues. The kids also needed counseling. We had to deal with the marriage, the drug addiction, the affair, the humiliation, and the issues brought on by both churches and childhood stuff.

The appointment was set a week later, and within that time Al had lost his job. It was only three weeks into our move to Atlanta and our new beginning. What was happening? This cannot be happening to us again, I thought. Now I knew we needed counseling. Al was back to doing his in-and-out routine. He was not coming home. He was stealing money out of our bank accounts, stealing and writing checks, and getting cash advances off the credit cards without my knowledge. I had to put a stop everything. I called the bank and reported the bank cards as stolen, as a means to get the money back. I could not begin to keep up with the lies because my kids were starting to see straight through them, although I had never said one word to them about anything. We would come home to an empty house; Al was stealing everything that he was able to carry.

Allyson was starting to act out in school almost every day. She was furious, and it came out in different ways. I was getting phone calls from a teacher a few times a week. Allyson has always been extremely verbal, and whereas Lauren's very subdued, but both were struggling, and they didn't even know why. I was only making matters worse because I didn't know how to explain to them what was happening. Al was their dad, their pastor, and their hero, all wrapped up in one. Lauren was hurting too, and although she was not verbal about it, I could see the pain in her eyes. She began to take on this false life of perfection. She strove to make everything perfect to keep from bringing me any more pain. She took on the task of becoming my "mini-me." At the age of thirteen, she was cleaning, cooking, washing, and assisting me with Allyson. She was still holding it all in and bearing the weight of all my pain without letting me know. She already knew the secret I had been keeping from them all this time, and I had no idea.

Oh God, I get to purge, I thought. I was so relieved. Finally, we are going to get some help! We were getting ready to see the executive pastor of this megachurch, and surely he would be able to help us through this understanding of our situation. Everything seemed to be in our favor. We found out Tiffany was not pregnant, and I thought, Hallelujah to that. It was all a lie! Al was home he had not been out binging. We were both equally excited about the fact that the help we had given to so many others was now about to be given to us.

We got to the church, and they took us to the executive pastor's office. I began to share our story, and from my assessment I had completed before this meeting, I could tell he knew the Bishop well but said he had only heard of Pastor Herman. After I was done telling my story and it was time for him to respond, there was a long pause. I was thinking, He is hearing from God, and he is about to give us a powerful word that would change our situation.

He said, "Wow, I know exactly what you all are going through." Because I am going through something similar.

I sat up in my seat with excitement, waiting for what else he had to say, surely, he can help us.

"There is nothing I can do for you. I am going through the same things myself and being honest with you; I shouldn't be counseling you."

He explained how he had just returned from a thirty-day, paid sabbatical. He was tired of ministry, and he was about to lose his mind and his family. His pastor sent him away to be restored.

He said, "Al, I understand because the only thing I haven't done is smoke crack. People don't understand what we go through in leadership." He paused. "At best, I can send Al to a twelve-step program here at the church, and, Alaina, you can come to some of the women programs here at the church. You can see what that does for you. I am sorry I can't help.

Please keep coming to church."

You have got to be kidding me. I must be getting punked. I thought as I began to look around for the cameras. We came to the church to get help, and now we have to leave the same way we came.

"This is the biggest church in Atlanta. Are you sure there is nothing more you can do for us? Can you send us to another pastor? You must be able to do something. We expected a plan of execution concerning what we can do to get better to mend our broken family. Again, after going through another counseling session, we're left more disappointed."

We sat in the parking lot and tried to figure out our next step. We no longer wanted to deal with the church at all. We figured we have been in the ministry so long and Al was a pastor so why not minister to ourselves. We went home and pulled out the books we used to counsel other couples. We felt so defeated. We had helped so many people in the past, but no one was able to help us. Al was so discouraged.

I began to pray and read my Bible.

I heard Al say, "I'll be back."

I heard the garage open, and he left.

CHAPTER 13

My Unforgettable Encounter

Al had yet another relapse. This time he was gone for six to seven days. I was scared to death because he had never been gone for that long. I found myself praying all night. I went on a fast in hopes God would deliver Al from this crack addiction. This particular night, after I had prayed, I could not sleep. It was around two o'clock in the morning, as I was flipping through the channels and I ran across Donnie McClurkin singing on Believer's Connection Network. I could not help but notice at the bottom of the screen it kept flashing, if you are in need of prayer call into this number. Normally, I would never call this number, but my husband had been gone for almost seven days. I was desperate, and I needed some assistance in this warfare we were fighting. I dialed the one-eight-hundred number, and a man with a Russian accent answered the phone.

"Thank you for calling BCN. What is your prayer request?" he asked.

"I am calling for you to pray with me for my husband who is a pastor. Well, he's a backslidden pastor."

"What is your name?" he asked in a polite voice.

"My name is Alaina."

"Well, what is going on with him?" he asked.

I said, "I need you to pray with me for his safe return home. He has been gone for seven days, and I am worried."

"Well, Alaina, what is his name?" he asked in a raspy growl with heavy breathing.

Although I was very emotional, I knew he was asking a bit much. I knew how a prayer line was supposed to work. Al had set up a prayer line for *The Church* in Cleveland, Ohio. You usually asked for the first name only and the need for the call. You say a short prayer and get off within sixty seconds, but I continued to answer the questions.

I said, "His name is Al."

Then I corrected myself and proceeded to give him Al's complete name. He continued breathing heavy and mumbling words. I did not understand quite what he was saying.

"Excuse me, but what are you saying?" I asked.

"Well, he is not a man of God," he said in that same tone of voice.

I was shocked, and I asked, "What? He is."

He became argumentative and abusive in his tone. I understood quickly that this was spiritual warfare.

I replied, "Satan, I rebuke you in the name of Jesus."

He yelled, "You! Let me tell you about you!"

I hung the phone up so fast because the call scared me to death. My heart was racing. I was so scared that I didn't know what to do. I realized I'd just had an encounter and conversation with the Devil. I got myself together and began to pray. I fell on the floor, and I pleaded for the blood of Jesus to cover my children, Al, and our lives. I got up off the floor and sat on my bed. I looked at the phone and contemplated if I should call back to BCN to tell them what I had just experienced or if I should call Pastor McCurry. It was much too early to call Pastor McCurry, so I hit the redial button to call BCN. I wanted to let them know what had just happened to me.

This time a sweet little old lady answered the phone with the same greeting as before.

I said, "Ma'am, I am not calling for a prayer request. I am calling to let you know what just happened."

I began to explain to her exactly what happened with the Russian man with a raspy voice answered the phone the last time I called.

She said, "I am so sorry."

"Ma'am, there is no need to apologize. It is ok. I was only calling to make you aware of what just happened to me."

She said, "I am apologizing because there are no men here tonight answering the phone. I can say a prayer for you."

"No men?" I replied.

"No, ma'am."

She said a short, sweet prayer with me, and then we got off the phone. I had to call Pastor McCurry, but it was only four-fifteen in the morning. I waited for time to pass because I didn't want to call her so early. To kill time, I watched the clock minute by minute and second by second until six a.m., and it finally came. I called her and told her what had happened to me when I called BCN. She told me that she needed to get her prayer warriors out, and she would call me back. She called me back a few hours later and said to me that Al would be ok. She said I would hear from him by two-thirty that afternoon. She explained to me, while she and her prayer warriors were interceding and praying for Al, they saw that the enemy was trying to take him out.

Al did call me at 2:15 p.m.

I asked him, "Where are you?"

He said, "I'm trying to get out, but this thing has a hold on me."

"Get out of where?" I asked.

"I'm headed that way, and I'll be home soon."

"Soon" turned into ten p.m. and considering everything I had just experienced earlier that day, when Al finally did get home, I had a million and one questions. He confirmed everything Pastor McCurry had told me over the phone. Now there are no churches, no counselors, and I still have not told my family about anything I was going through here in Atlanta. The only other person that knew anything was Mona. I had to stop talking to her because since I had been gone, I found out she was going back and telling Pastor Herman and the leadership everything. I know this to be true because I confronted her about it, and she admitted to it. She said the only reason she told them was because they were concerned and wanted to pray for me. Mona knew better. She knew that they did not like me, nor were they concerned about me.

I did not have time to try to figure out why she was doing this. At this moment, I knew my relationship with her was not right, and it had to be put on pause. Just like that, I hit the delete button and removed her from my life. Now I didn't have anyone else to talk to. I was on the brink of a nervous breakdown. I was trying to carry the weight of the world on my shoulders all alone. I realized it was at this time, that God was intentionally isolating me from my family, the church, and my friends. With the help of Pastor McCurry via phone long distance, this was when I learned how to war in the spirit.

"For we wrestle not against flesh and blood but the principalities, against powers, against the rulers of the darkness of this world, against spiritual wickedness in high places," the Bible says in Ephesians 6:12.

CHAPTER 14

Hurt People Hurt People

Al was in a ninety-day rehab program, and I was watching church on TV. I was pouring my all into my girls and work as I tried to build my clientele because I was the only one working at this point. I had left JCPenney because I had a set schedule there and I needed to have a more flexible schedule to be there for my girls and to get them where they needed to be. I found a salon close to my house and began to rent a booth. I worked very hard to build a clientele, but it was no comparison to the money I had been accustomed to making. Money was tight, and my savings were gone. I was struggling to pay the bills, and I could no longer afford the house or the new cars we had. The repo man was coming to take the truck, and we were getting eviction notices on the door. At one point, it got so bad that we didn't have any gas or running water, so I had to resort to desperate measures. I would steal water from the salon I worked at when the owner left. I would fill up twenty-five-gallon water containers that I had stored in my trunk to use for cooking, drinking, bathing, and keeping my car running because of a broken radiator. We would drive for a few miles and then have to pull over on the side of the road. The car would overheat, and smoke would fill the front that I could not even see. I could not afford to pay for a replacement because I drove a 745i BMW, and everything was expensive to fix.

Life was tough. I had never heard of having to pay for garbage collection. In Cleveland, you put your garbage on the front lawn, and the city picked it up. Not in Atlanta. We had to pay, and eventually, I could no longer afford it. I would allow the garbage to stack up, and then my girls and I would load the garbage up in the trunk of my car. We would drive in the dark with the lights off and looked for homes where it appeared the residents were sleeping. Then we would quickly unload our garbage onto their lawns and jump back into the car and pull off fast.

Al would get jobs off and on, but I would never receive the money because it all went to his drug addiction. I'd been looking for somewhere else to live because of the eviction notice, but the eviction came faster than the new place. After days of searching, we were finally evicted from our dream home, and everything we owned was on the front lawn. Here I was humiliated and embarrassed as everyone was riding down the street, looking. I finally had a meltdown. I began rolling on the ground from the driveway to the grass in disbelief. God, why are you allowing me to go through this? I hadn't asked for any of this. We had met a fantastic family--Ma Betsy and her husband, whom we affectionately called "Ma and Dad.' They took us in as their children. We would have Bible studies at their home. They helped me get a U-Haul truck and movers. We loaded the truck and stayed with them for a few nights until I was approved for my apartment.

*****

Now I'd moved four times while in Atlanta. We had gone from a six-figure income to be receiving welfare, food stamps, and Medicaid.

One evening as I was in the kitchen preparing the water for Allyson's bath, she asked, "Mommy, does anyone in Cleveland know what we're going through like Pastor Herman and the people from *The Church*? What about Bishop and his wife? Have they called to see how we're doing? They're supposed to be our godparents."

Allyson was eleven and a half years old, and she was wise beyond her years.

I said, "Yes, they know some things, and, no, they have not called to check on us. Allyson, we're God's responsibility, not theirs. I know it does not seem like we are ever going to get out of this, but we are. When we do, no one will be able to take credit but God."

"Mommy, why did Daddy work so hard at *"The Church."* He was always there for everybody--" She started to mumble something I could not understand, and then she said, "No one can help us."

I didn't know how to respond to that because I felt the same way, not so much about Pastor Herman, but about Bishop and his wife. They never called once to see if we were ok or if we needed anything. I had helped them at the Pentecostal Church and their home and absolutely nothing. They went from buying my girls clothes from Sak's Fifth Avenue to nothing. I had to remind myself what I shared with Allyson always: we are God's responsibility.

It was the summer before Lauren's junior year of high school. I could not take it anymore. I had been bearing all of this alone. I had to talk to someone, so I finally reached out to my mother and told her everything I had been going through while here in Atlanta. She could not believe her ears.

She said, "I knew something was wrong, but I would never have imagined it was to this magnitude."

She burst into tears. Although my mom was hurt, she could relate because she had suffered silently with my dad. It wasn't even a week later, and my mom called and told me that she would be here in Atlanta with me and my girls on Friday. She walked away from everything she had built in Cleveland. She packed up her sixty-seven-year-old self, some clothes, and her car. Then she told my sister and brother to pack up the rest of her things that were left and then to put her house on the market to sell. She told them she was going to Atlanta to see her daughter.

****

I needed a refuge, and the only place where I knew to get one was from the church. TV just was not getting it anymore. I needed to be there in the spirit. I decided to look for a new church home. I heard a new church was coming to the city that was not far from where I lived. I was a little apprehensive because I had never heard of the pastor, but I had followed his wife. I had admired her dearly and followed her ministry for years. Once the church was done, and Sunday came, the girls and I were ready. I was a pro at church. I could spot anything that was out of order, who was in charge, who was trying to be significant, and who was important. I was trained like that. This behavior kept me distracted and sometimes made it hard to embrace what God was trying to say to me. I became very critical, judgmental and now hurt, which was not a good mixture.

This time, I was going to be open and not look for anything wrong. I would always sit in the front because I hated to sit in the back. We got to church early so I could get a good seat. I'd heard this church would be packed. As we walked in, the greeters met us and welcomed us to Destiny Church. Everyone was so nice.

One of the greeters asked me, "Will your children be attending the youth church?"

I looked at my children, and before I could ask them, they both said yes. I signed them in and proceeded to the main sanctuary. It was a breath of fresh air! Everyone I encountered operated in excellence, the parking attendants, the greeters, the youth church workers, and even the ushers. Ushers could sometimes be so mean, nasty and could turn you completely off from the church. Not here, because you could tell they had been trained well. They were very mature and sharp. This stood out to me, because if the leadership and the workers were like this, then the pastor had to be on point. That's who they received their instruction from or who set the atmosphere of the house.

As I waited for service to start, I was greeted by several people. They said things like, "Welcome to Destiny, we're so delighted you are visiting with us," and, "You're in for a treat." I felt they were genuine and down to earth. I didn't know what to expect, but I must admit I was blown away. This was a new ministry, and the pastor was not from Atlanta. He was from Washington, DC, and I'd heard when he moved there, he had bought several people with him. I was impressed. It is 9:58 a.m. when the praise team took the stage, and at ten o'clock on the dot, the worship service began. Oh my, the energy was so hype. They had that DC feel, and it was amazing. After the first song, in comes this well-put-together man. I mean, he was put together from head to toe. He was immaculate. He looked to be well educated and somewhat distinguished, with his wireframes and paisley bowtie.

In my critical mind, I thought, oh boy, I sure hope he's not boring. I needed a word, and I didn't come for any games. I looked to see his wife, but she was not there. I didn't care because I was looking for God. I was broken and needed to hear from Him.

As I worshiped, I could feel the presence of God. The pastor walked to the pulpit alone. There was no security and no armor-bearers.

I thought, Wow this is different. He continued to worship and greeted everyone. It was running very smoothly. It was time for the word. This man was no joke. Just as I'd thought, he was educated, but he was also very easy to follow. He didn't use the pulpit to curse anyone or air anyone's dirty laundry, nor did he talk about his wife, kids, dogs, or cats. He gave me what I came for, and that was a Word for what I was going through. I felt so empowered. After service was over, he came down to greet everyone. There was still no security or a gang of people telling you that you could not talk to him. I must admit I was blown away. Now if only the girls had the same experience, I could genuinely see myself coming back. As I left the sanctuary and headed to get my children, I saw they were not finished. I stood in the back and waited. They had a real church for the youth. The altar was full, and the kids were so sincere. They finally came out, and the youth pastor saw that Lauren and Allyson were with me. He spoke to me and told me he honestly enjoyed having them there today. Then he asked them in front of me if they enjoyed the service. They both said yes, and then he told us to have a great week.

As we walked to the car, they could not stop talking about how much they learned. Lauren loved the worship and the word. Allyson was more focused on the presentation and the fact she learned something. I was so glad they enjoyed it. Al would soon be released from his ninth rehab. I couldn't wait for our hour phone call that night. I told him about our experience at the church, and he was excited to hear about it. Al was coming home next week. He wasn't going to finish his full time there because he felt he had gotten all he needed. Al always felt that he knew more than the counselors. He had started rehab programs at both of our previous churches, and he was responsible for countless people getting free from drugs because of his testimony.

He came home on Tuesday, and we went to Bible study as a family on Wednesday. Al was blown away just as I was. When service was over, I told Al I was going to get the girls. We waited for Al to come out, but we did not see him. I asked myself, what is taking him so long? I knew he couldn't have left because I had the keys. I didn't trust Al even to hold the keys. I walked back to the sanctuary, and I saw Al on the altar talking to Bishop Strong. I then saw him pray for Al. Afterward, they beckoned for one the elders of the church to join them, and they talked a little while longer. The elder walked with Al to the back, and then Al introduced me to him. The elder told me, "I look forward to seeing you next week."

As Al and I walked to the car, he explained to me that after service, he'd walked to the front and approached Bishop Strong to introduce himself. He said he'd told him that he was Elder Carpenter and he was a backslidden preacher. He explained to Bishop Strong that he needed help with his family and that we had been here for three years. He told the bishop that we had gone to other churches and counselors and we were still struggling. Al explained everything that had happened and who he worked for back in Cleveland. Bishop Strong knew Bishop very well and said they were going to help. He told Al he would have one of his elders contact him to set up a time for Al and me to meet with him and his wife. He told Al everything would be kept confidential. I was ecstatic because I loved his wife. She was so powerful!

I asked, "Al, do you want help?"

This was so out of his character. The next week came, and just like the pastor promised, the elder called to set up the meeting. He explained that Bishop Strong's wife was out of the country and Bishop Strong was back in DC. He didn't want us to wait any longer, so he and his wife would meet with us, and Al agreed. They set up a time for us to meet, and the elder asked Al if he had ever heard of Pappadeaux's restaurant. Al told him yes but that we had never been. They set it up for the meeting to take place there.

As Al explained the conversation, I asked, "Why are we going to a restaurant? We need counseling, not a business meeting. This does not seem like it's going to be good."

Alaina, you need to be a little more optimistic, I thought.

The day had come for us to meet. I woke up feeling good that day. Al had been home a full week, and there was no drinking or getting high. He had even stopped smoking cigarettes. Could this be our new beginning? I asked myself.

Our reservations were at 7:00 p.m., so we got ready and arrived at around six fifty. Al texted them to let them know that we were there. The elder replied and said for us to go ahead and be seated because they were running a few minutes behind. As we waited, we talked. It was our first time out to dinner in a while.

Well, maybe this restaurant thing was not such a bad idea, after all, I thought. The elder and his wife finally arrived. As they approached us, Al stood up to greet them. We hugged, and they sat down. The elder told us that this was one of his favorite restaurants. He also explained that Bishop Strong wanted to be there, but because of his schedule, he could not attend.

"Please order whatever you would like. This is on Bishop. He is paying for this. You must try my favorite appetizer: shrimp and crawfish fondeaux," the Elder said. He wanted to make sure that you both had a good time."

What good time? We need counseling! Ok, be optimistic, Alaina, remember? They ordered several appetizers and beverages. As we were waiting for the appetizers to come out, the elder asked us to tell him a little about ourselves. He wanted to know where we came from, what we did in our previous church, so forth, and so on. Al began to tell them about our roles at both churches in Cleveland. I wished Al had not done have that.

The elder said, "Wow, you all were high up. I know of both of your former pastors."

His wife kept looking at me to see if would say something. Finally, we ordered our main dish, and the appetizers came out so now we were eating. The elder tucked his bib around his neck and was eating like he had not eaten in days. He was a big guy, and he was putting a hurting on this food.

I thought, "When the Bishop gets this bill, I sure hope he doesn't think we ate like this." I was sitting there getting frustrated because this was not going as I thought it would. Did anyone hear us say that we need help? The elder's wife could see that I was not feeling this because I barely ate any of my food.

She said, "Lady Carpenter--"

I interrupted and said, "Please call me Alaina."

I knew early on that I would not allow people to put my family and me on a pedestal. I understood that we were servants of God and that this was not a glamorous position, and I never wanted to lose sight of that. I never let anyone call me that, even when we pastored our church.

She said, "You look so nice tonight. Your hair is sharp!"

Ok, here we go. Why is she kissing up to me? I hate when women do that. What's next? I thought.

"You're so quiet. Is everything ok?" she asked.

"No, everything is not ok," I stated. "We wanted to meet with you for counseling and because we need help. I am dying because my husband is on crack, and we are sitting here like we are being interviewed for a job. Why are we here? I know church and pastors like the back of my hand. I've been doing this for over twenty-plus years. I don't mean to come off abrasive, but if you can't counsel us, let us know now."

At this point, from the conversation that had already taken place, we should have been counseling them. All he did was talk about Bishop Strong and his wife, how powerful they were, that Bishop Strong was going to bring him on to the ministry full-time, and how they were looking for influential leaders to help. I thought, oh hell no, if this is going where I think it is.

The elder explained how he had been on drugs and how he'd gotten off. He told us that he started helping others in ministry and that God took the appetite for drugs away, and now he had been serving for seven years. He said that he was the head elder of this ministry.

So what, I thought. How is your bio helping us?

He said, "Al, I think you both should get back in ministry."

It began to wake up that desire that was familiar with in Al, but I had to bring some reality to the table.

"Maybe you didn't hear us. We are sick I had to spell it out S I C K sick and need help. I can't minister to anyone because I hate church people right now. I'm like a venomous snake if I open my mouth; I am liable to hurt them more than help them. Just in case you have forgotten, Al is struggling with crack. He's not fit to help himself. He doesn't even have sixty days clean."

This is what is wrong with the church now. We have hurting and insecure pastors, first ladies and ministers in leadership hurting other people. They leave one church wounded and go to start or join another without getting the proper healing needed to move on. I didn't want to be like that. I truly wanted to be free of all the rage, pain, bitterness, guilt, embarrassment, and unforgiveness so that I could one day help someone else. Today was not that day.

After I said what I had to say, Elder said, "Wow, you are a powerful woman of God. You remind me of Bishop Strong's wife."

I thought "This man has rocks for a brain." He was so caught up with titles and kissing butt that he could not see the forest for the trees. Although I admired Bishop Strong's wife, I was not at all swayed by the comparison. I squeezed Al's leg under the table to say it was time to end this meeting. I thought "This couple is sicker than us."

Al said, "Thanks for dinner, but we need to get home to our children."

The waiter brought the bill, and the elder paid it.

As we walked to the parking lot, the elder asked, "Can I pray for you two?"

We said, "Yes."

When he was done with the prayer, we all said Amen.

Elder's wife said, "Alaina, here is my phone number. If you ever need anyone to talk to or pray with, call me."

I said, "Ok."

Al and Elder were still talking. I went and sat in the car. When I closed the door, I took the slip of paper with her phone number on it, balled it up, and threw it away. I said, "I won't be needing this."

Al finally got in the car and asked, "What did you think? You were so on point with what you said because we are sick, but they are too."

We both busted out laughing.

I said, "I was thinking the same thing at the table."

"What's that saying?" he asked

At the same time, we said, "Hurt people hurt people!"

Although we did not continue the counseling sessions, we continued to go to the church. It was there that the girls and I received our healing. Al did well for about two months. Then he relapsed again, and it was off to another rehab. This time he finished his ninety days and got this bright idea for us to start a Bible study. Some way, I fell for it, and we did. Al was an amazing preacher and teacher. I had never sat under a pastor who taught the word like him. We were still attending Destiny Church. The girls were very active. After being there for around nine months or so, rumors began to fly that Bishop Strong and his wife were having problems. It was causing a rift in the ministry.

Now our Bible study turned into a full-blown church called God's House. I didn't want to do it, but it was the longest Al had been clean, which was approximately four months, and the church was growing. Maybe the elder was right about getting into ministry. Everything was going well. My mom was there, and we were doing ministry again. Our kids were thriving. Lauren had received a record deal, and she had been on Tyler Perry's House of Payne. She was performing all over Atlanta. Allyson was playing basketball all over the city. She had a personal trainer who was a former NBA player for the Milwaukee Bucks. We were now heading in the right direction. One night after Bible study, I received a phone call from a private number. I usually didn't answer those calls, but this time I did.

"Hello," I said.

I could barely understand what the person was saying because she was crying and trying to talk at the same time.

"She has cancer! Alaina, please pray for me!"

I caught the voice, and it was Mona.

"Who has cancer?"

"Grandma! Oh no!"

Mona knew how much I loved her grandmother and her father.

I began to pray, and said, "Father in the name of Jesus--"

When I finished praying for her, I began to ask questions.

"When did you find out? What are the doctors saying? How is your father? Is she receiving chemo? How have you been?"

I had so many questions to ask. I had not spoken to her in forever. When I finally calmed down, I noticed that Mona was slurring her words.

She said, "Grandma had surgery three weeks ago, and they got all cancer out."

"What? Then why did you call me acting like she was at death's door? I'm finishing up something, so I will have to call you back."

She said, "Please don't forget because I have to tell you something."

I quickly realized that she only did that to reconnect with me. I missed her, so I wanted to catch up with her and the family. As we headed home, from Bible study, I told Al what had just happened with Mona. Al told me to be careful with Mona. He had never said that before in all the years that we had been friends

"What are you talking about?" I asked.

He said, "Don't forget why you stopped talking to her in the first place."

"Al, I'm not crazy."

I waited until the next morning before I called her. We talked on the phone for almost two hours. I finally had some good news about my family. There was Al's clean time, Lauren's record deal and appearance on Tyler Perry's House of Payne, and the church we had started. My clientele had picked up. I was doing better financially, and we were on an upswing.

"How are you doing?" she asked.

"I'm ok. How are your daughter and husband?" I asked

"They're good," she answered, and it was obvious that she missed me as I missed her.

Mona didn't have any real friends, but I was one. People loved to be around her because she knew so many people and was always in the limelight. If you needed a connection or a spectacular event, she was the one to go to. Mona was a beast at what she did. I didn't want anything from Mona. We were just great friends. As we were about to get off the phone, she said that we would stay connected.

She also said, "Alaina, I am sorry for betraying your trust. I will never do that again. I thought they were concerned for you."

"How is that going for you? Are you still working for Pastor Herman?"

She replied, "Yes, but Lady Herman and her secret servicewomen hate my guts. They are so messy. I know just what you were going through. Not on the same level, but I sure get it. I have to deal with them by myself because you're gone. I am so glad that Pastor Herman doesn't pay his wife's opinion any mind. Between getting surgeries and having babies, she doesn't have time to be in my business anyway."

I was shocked, and asked, "Surgeries? Mona, really?"

"Yep, surgeries."

"How do you know all that?" I asked.

"I gave her a few of my doctor friends' information."

"Girl TMI. Just forget it because I don't even want to know," I told her while shaking my head.

"She's pregnant again and consumed and focused on trying to keep this baby."

I said, "Wow, she's pregnant again. That's crazy. That is so risky," I replied.

She was trying to bring me into this conversation. For me, it was too much information. I was so far removed from them that I was not even interested. I had been gone away from them for three years now, and I could not care less about anything that was going on with them.

"I will be praying for you," I said as we ended our conversation and got off the phone.

It felt really good to talk to her. It was like old times again. We began to talk every day.

We were almost six months in, and to Al being clean, and every day I was thanking God. We took a trip back to Cleveland, and Al suggested that we go and visit "The Church." I didn't want to go, but I went anyway. It was a Friday afternoon. We pulled up at *The Church* I tried to talk Al from going because I didn't have a good feeling.

I said, "Al, I'm not going in."

He said, "Ok, I won't be long."

He went in, and the girls and I stayed in the car. After fifteen minutes, my phone rang, and it was Mona.

"Where are you?" she asked.

"I'm in the car."

"Girl, when I saw Al, I was like I know Alaina is here. Why didn't you tell me you were coming to Cleveland?"

BEHIND CHURCH DOORS

She was talking to me and coming to the parking lot at the same time. Mona was the type that had to know everything about everybody. She came out to the car and hugged me.

"I'm killing you. You could have told me you were coming here. I wouldn't have told anyone. Come in the church. Everyone is here. Lady Herman is here, and they want to see you and the girls."

I'm asking myself, why is Mona so happy about me seeing Lady Herman? This is the same person she said hated her. Did she forget that she just talked about her to me? That was Mona, so we reluctantly got out the car and went in. Mona was so happy. She took us around to see everyone. It looked different inside. They had remolded "The Church." We ended up in Lady Herman's office.

"Hey, Sister Carpenter," Lady Herman said with a giggle.

We hugged and talked for about ten minutes or so. After that, in walked Al and Pastor Herman.

I said, "Hello."

Pastor Herman was noticeably uncomfortable with my presence.

"Hey, Sister Carpenter." As he quickly left, he said, "Al, stay in touch and have a safe trip back."

We all hugged and said our good-byes.

Lady Herman and Mona walked us outside. I could see Mona walking us out but not Lady Herman.

"Ok, I see y'all in the 745 Beamer," Lady Herman said.

I thought, Really? They are still shallow as ever. She didn't say anything like wow y'all are still together, y'all made it, congratulations on Lauren's record deal, or we saw her on House of Payne. I knew that they knew about those things because Mona called me and asked if she could tell the Hermans about my girls. She promised me that she would not mention anything about Al or me. She said she wanted to irritate Lady Herman anyway. They hated for anyone to have or do anything better than them. They thought they were the only people that good things were supposed to happen to, or they had to be the facilitators who made it happen for someone else.

We laughed, and I'd said, "Mona, you are a fool. Yeah, you can go ahead and tell them that."

As we pulled out the parking lot, I asked, "Al, how do you feel?"

He had this crazy, blank stare on his face.

He replied, "I'm cool."

"What did you and Herman talk about?"

It took him a minute to answer. It was as if he was processing their conversation.

He finally said, "He has not changed a bit. Can you believe this man told me how much the church had grown and how the elder who took my place was now making six figures? He had built a new home. The meeting was all about what he had, see what you left; I was setting you up for this. He told me he was going to give me a church if I had stayed. I'm the one who executed his million-dollar plan."

Now let me take you all back.

The Church had begun to grow fast, and Pastor Herman had always been in fear of losing it in the beginning. He had been determined to remain secure in his finances. He said he could not worry about giving the people God's Word and still worry about having enough money to take care of his family and pay his bills. He had come up with a plan to become a millionaire within one year. He had Al, his secretaries, and finance team go through the list of the top contributors to the church. They had figured out what it would take to earn a million dollars by having those members to do a pledge. Then Al had put together this elaborate banquet where they would recognize and honor the top contributors of "The Church." At the end of the banquet, they had been given pledge cards to pledge "The Church," which was really for the pastor.

The day of the event, Al had set it up, but he refused to show up because he had felt horrible for his participation in that foolishness. Pastor Herman was not happy about Al's absence. He didn't raise the million dollars, but he did raise around six hundred thousand or so. It had been a few weeks later that Al had been removed as executive pastor to director of sports ministry. Pastor Herman moved Al to an empty office in the gym and had been told to figure it out because *The Church* was not spending another dime on office furniture. Pastor Herman was so cold and cutthroat. Is this how he repaid Al for not coming to the banquet or for not raising the million dollars?

The office was more extensive than his previous office, with not even a chair. Al was really hurt. He could not believe he was being treated so harshly after he had given so much of himself. Thank God for Floyd Swoope.

Floyd was a business owner in Cleveland. He had owned a chain of salons as well as his own hair-care line. He also owned a computer and office furniture store. Floyd had not been known for going to church; he was a street guy.

I loved Floyd. He had given me my first job when I'd been fourteen years old as a shampoo assistant at one of his salons. Floyd was true to his word. He had been true to the streets, his business, and his family. So when Floyd decided to join "The Church," he had been faithful to that as well. He was a part of Al's new member's class, and they'd hit it off well. Floyd had not been a fan of Herman because of business dealings he'd had with him. Al continued to talk to Floyd, encouraging him not to leave the ministry. When Floyd had found out what Pastor Herman had done to Al, he was mad as hell. Mona told Floyd what Herman had done. Floyd furnished Al's entire office with brand-new furniture along with a desktop and laptop computer. Floyd thought the whole thing was some

BS. He told Al that niggas don't get down like this in the streets, and he was supposed to be a man of God.

"Man, I promise if it were not for you, I would have already left this church," Floyd had said to Al.

When Herman had heard that Al had gotten his office together, he had come over to see it.

He asked Al, "Where did you get all this from?"

Al had said, "Floyd Swoope blessed me with it."

"Really? I'm going to have to order me some new furniture. Your office looks better than mine," Pastor Herman had stated.

Back in the car driving home with Al, I said, "I knew we should have never come here. One day you are going to listen to me."

He asked, "Do you know what is crazy?"

"What?" I asked.

"When Herman heard your voice in the hallway, he began to try to rush me out. It was like he was scared or something."

"Really? What was that all about?"

"I noticed that he was uncomfortable in his wife's office," I said.

We were leaving early the next morning. Al was acting very different after his visit with Pastor Herman. Maybe it was because he was not working and had a struggling ministry in Atlanta. When we were members of "The Church," Pastor Herman would always throw in Al's face a reminder of what he was paying him. When we arrived back to Atlanta, Al still could not shake that visit with Pastor Herman. After being back in Atlanta for three days, his six months clean time ended, and he relapsed again. This was one of the worst relapses yet. He was gone for eight days. He had taken everything that he could. When I came home, it was like we had been robbed. Lauren's laptop, Allyson PlayStation, the microwave, the radios, and the DVD players were all gone. I was out done.

I could not do this another day. I had finally had enough. He had to go far away. He had already gone to nineteen rehabs in Atlanta and two in Florida. I didn't care where he went, but he had to get away from here. I called his mother and father to explain what was going on and that I needed their help with their son. I explained to them that I wanted to find a program far away because I couldn't do this anymore. His mother knew of every drug rehab in the country. She had assisted several of her family members on getting into treatment centers. She called me to let me know that she had found one in Houston, Texas. She called and made the arrangements, but they needed to speak to him directly. He still had not returned home. I began to pray and pack all his stuff. It was the weekend of the Fourth of July in 2008. Now I had moved for the fourth time, but this time, he was not on the lease, and I had the upper hand, or so I thought.

One day the girls and I returned home, and to our surprise, he was there. It scared the mess out of me because he did not have a key to this apartment, but he was home.

I walked in our room, and I asked, "How did you get in here?"

"I had the maintenance man let me in. Why?" he asked.

"Because you don't have a key," I blurted out.

He was pissed off and asked, "Why are my clothes packed up?"

"Really? Because you can't stay here any longer. I can't do this anymore. Your mother has found a rehab in Houston, Texas."

"Houston? I'm not going to no damn Houston," he said with a defiant attitude.

"That will be your choice, but you cannot stay here."

I called his mother to let her know what was going on.

"He's back, and he is saying he is not going, so you can send him a one-way ticket back to Cleveland."

She replied, "Oh no, we're already dealing with two crackheads here. They are trying to kill us."

"I'm sorry to hear that, but he has to go because I'm not going to allow him to kill me," I told her.

She said, "Wait until in the morning. Let him get some sleep, and we will deal with this in the morning."

After I got off the phone with his mother, I told my girls that their daddy would be going to Texas for a year. I wanted them to know although he was staying here tonight he would be leaving soon. They were happy that he was moving. They were tired of all the drama and leaving in constant fear. They had been through so much by this time.

The next morning arrived.

Al woke up and asked, "Can we talk?"

I said, "Yes."

He said, "Ok, explain the program."

"Here is the number, so call it. Your mother set this up. You have two days to be here; then you have to go!" I told him in a demanding tone.

He tried to fight calling the center, but he realized that I was not playing this time. When he called the rehab in Houston, the intake person asked for his information, and Al gave it to him.

The intake person asked, "Are you from Atlanta?"

Al replied, "I live in Atlanta, but I am from Cleveland, Ohio."

"Is this the Al Carpenter who played ball for JFK?" the intake person asked with a bit of glee in his voice.

Al asked, "Yeah, who is this?"

"Man, this is Wayne Seals from Shaw High School."

What were the chances that the counselor all the way in Houston, Texas, would be from Cleveland, and that they knew each other? This had to be a sign from God. Al agreed to leave. His mother and I moved fast to make this happen. The next night his bus left at 11:00 p.m. Al was very concerned about being gone for nine months to a year.

He asked, "Are you going to divorce me?"

I said, "Al, if you do what you're supposed to do, then no. I want my family but not like this. The only thing you should be worried about is getting better."

The next day came, and he spent it with the girls. Then later that evening I took him to the bus stop. He had been drinking, and I was so scared that he was not going to get on the bus.

He said, "You can leave."

"Not until I see the bus pull off with you on it!"

"Let me get ten dollars so I can eat at the stops," he asked.

It was an eighteen-hour bus ride.

I said, "I've packed your food and drinks in a cooler, so you'll be fine. I have all your favorites."

I was prepared.

He asked, "Do you want me gone that bad?"

"I really want you clean."

He boarded the bus. I gave him five dollars for an emergency. I called his mother to let her know that he was on the bus.

She said, "Don't leave until that bus pulls off. He might try to get off of it."

I told her, "I'm not going anywhere. He was trying to get me to give him ten dollars."

"Did you give it to him?"

I said, "No, I gave him five."

"He didn't tell you we sent him fifty dollars today?"

I yelled, "What! Why would you do that? I wondered how he had money to get something to drink. You're trying to kill him. You and your husband have been feeding his addiction for the last three years. If you want just to blow some money, your grandkids could use it, seeing that you had not done anything for them, not one dime!"

I wanted to go off even more, but now I had to watch the bus leave, so he would not get off. You talk about being scared to death. However, the bus did its final call, and it slowly pulled out. I ran and got in my car and followed it to 85 to make sure he was still on the bus. I was exhausted. I went home and passed out. It was the first time I had slept all night in a while.

It was Lauren's senior year of high school. She still had her record deal, and Allyson still had her busy basketball schedule. Allyson was raising brows of scouts from different private schools. Now that Al was gone, my mom felt like we were doing better. Now she could return to Cleveland and resume some normalcy in her life. I was grateful for the year and a half that she sacrificed for my children and me. I truly did not want to see her leave, and my kids were so sad. That was the only grandmother that they had in their lives, and they were very close. My siblings came and packed her up.

My brother said, "Alaina, you don't have to stay here alone. Let us take you back to Cleveland."

I said, "No, it's Lauren's last year, and I want her to finish high school with her friends."

With tears in his eyes, he said, "Ok."

They all were very concerned about me. My family never said one bad thing about Al to my girls or me. They just wanted us safe.

Now it was back to life that was only about my girls and me. We could finally enjoy Atlanta with no interruptions and some peace, which was something that we had not had in a while. We got word from Wayne that Al had made it safely and he was doing well. I was relieved.

CHAPTER 15

Motives

Everything was going well. Lauren was doing great with her record deal. She was performing all over Atlanta. Allyson was doing phenomenal in basketball, and she had been accepted into one of the top private schools in Atlanta. I was working at one of the most popular salons in Duluth, Georgia, called Shyne Hair Studio. We were finally back on the right track. Things were going great, but I was missing my mom. Talking to my sister, Mona, and my friends Tracie and Kim on the phone every day about what was going on in Cleveland was making me yearn to be back there. A couple of weeks went by, and then Mona called me, sounding very disturbed. She informed me that Pastor Herman had fired her. I could not believe it, and neither could she. She had given up a stable, high-paying job to come and work for Pastor Herman.

I said, "Are you kidding me? Did he give you a reason, or did he just fire you like that? Did you say something wrong or were you stealing?"

I started bombarding her with a bunch of questions.

She said, "It had to be Pastor Herman's wife and her crazy armor-bearers because you know they hated me, but then again, he fired the entire staff. It was all of us, about five or six." He had just recently hired a new CFO, and it was his recommendation.

"Are you ok?"

She said, "I don't know what I'm gone do."

She sounded so broken. I had never heard Mona sound like that before. That sound was so familiar...

"You're so smart, and you have your bachelor's and master's degrees. A job shouldn't be anything for you. You know plenty of people. You're the one that got Pastor Herman connected."

Now Mona was the type of person that hated to lose, and she always had to be seen on her A game. You would never see her sweat. She always had to be on top because she worked hard to get there and even harder to maintain it at any cost. Mona was devastated, so I was trying to be there for her. I did not want her to have the feeling of loneliness that I had experienced, so I was there for her as she had been there for me.

After weeks and weeks of talking to Mona, it was now November, and I got a call from Wayne in Houston, Texas. He said Al was done with his ninety-day rehab program and had been released to a transitional home. He left the house and had relapsed again. He was living on the streets of Houston, and Wayne had went and found him.

I thought this is too much. I was just glad that I was in Atlanta and he was in Texas. I couldn't handle that all over again. I made up in my mind that I was not going through this again. I began to pray and went on a fast to get direction from the Lord because I could not live another day dealing with his addiction and I wanted a divorce. I called Pastor McCurry, we prayed, and I felt a release. The very next day I went online and pulled paperwork on how I could file for a divorce with Al in Texas and me in Atlanta.

In February 2009, my divorce was final. I had divorced Al and never even told him. He had no idea that we were no longer married.

One day I was talking to Mona, and out of nowhere, I said, "Mona, I want to come home."

Mona asked, "Are you serious? Alaina, do not play with me. Come on home! We can open up a business together and turn the city of Cleveland out."

I said, "Mona, this is too much. I can't believe I just said this to you. I have to call you back."

I hung up the phone, and then I waited for my girls to get home from school. I sat them down and asked them how they felt about us moving back home to Cleveland after Lauren's graduation in May, and they began screaming. When I saw the reaction of my girls, I knew this would be the right move. I called my sister and informed her that I was coming home.

She asked, "When are you coming home?"

I said, "The day after Lauren's graduation."

She just broke down crying. I ended that call, and then I called Mona back. I informed her that I was for sure coming home, and she was pumped. We began to talk about building a salon. Although we loved one another, we were both apprehensive about going into business together. It was more me than her. I explained to her that I did not like the way that she did business. I felt that she was cutthroat, shrewd, and abrasive in how she handled people. I didn't want my name associated with that in business. My other concern was she was always concerned about the bottom line. She began to explain to me that her concerns with me were that I was a flip-flopper, and when I didn't want to do something, I hid behind my kids and Al. I explained to her why, but we decided to partner together and open the hottest salon in Cleveland.

Mona was determined to show the Herman's that she would be back on top and that she knew how to run a salon, considering the salon that *The Church* opened had failed. That was Mona. She always had an ulterior motive, unlike me, because I could care less about the Herman's. They were nonfactors in my life; the damage had already been done. In a matter of two and a half months, we put together a full-fledged salon, and we did it all while I was still in Atlanta. Mona did all the legwork.

She found three potential places. She sent me pictures, and we talked over the phone. I was to find all the equipment, all while I was looking for Allyson a private school and planning for Lauren's graduation party back in Cleveland. This was so much fun. This was also keeping my mind occupied so I would not have to think about Al. My girl and I would be back together again.

CHAPTER 16

Moving Day

It was graduation day, May 24, 2009, and we were filled with so much emotion. Lauren graduated at the top of her class with an honors diploma, and she was named the student of the year. She was accepted to Savannah State University, Savannah College of Art and Design, and Kent State University. Allyson graduated from middle school. She was in the gifted-and-talented program and came out with awards in practically every subject. It amazed me that my kids were able to achieve so much, even in the midst of all we had gone through. We were so happy, yet sad, because Al was not in attendance at her graduation. He had missed everything her record deal, her TV debut. His absence is something that became very familiar. She graduated with honors and was voted the Student of the Year award for the entire Gwinnett County and without fail my whole family came down for this joyous occasion.

I had given away everything I owned to my shampoo assistant. I furnished her whole apartment. I packed up in the U-Haul with what was left. I cleaned the apartment and then drove the truck to the hotel where we would be spending our last night in Georgia. We made it back to Cleveland on May 25, and I only had $236 to my name after paying for the U-Haul, gas, and food during our ride back. We also had no place of our own to live. We moved in with my sister until I could get back on my feet. Lauren's graduation party was well attended. Lauren received over three thousand dollars in cash and seven hundred dollars in gift cards, and that is how we survived for the next few weeks.

The next Sunday, we decided we would go and visit our old Pentecostal church. We thought we had walked into a time warp. It was good to see everybody, but it was the same. Everyone was saying the same thing as if they were stuck and time had stood still. There was no growth. It was very obvious that we had grown leaps and bounds and that my walk with Christ was no longer contingent on a building or flesh. I had experienced a true relationship with God, and I now knew Him for myself. After visiting my old church, neither my girls nor I wanted to be there. Still wounded, I didn't trust anyone. I decided to take a break from church, and I poured everything into building the salon.

CHAPTER 17

The Friendship

Mona was so excited for us to be working together again. Building this salon was a dream of hers since the age of eighteen. Mona and I met when I was in the eleventh grade. We'd become friends in cosmetology school. It was an instant connection. Mona was always so much fun. She had gone to high school with my cousins, so we knew a lot of the same people, which made the connection even more comfortable. After really getting to know Mona, I'd realized that we'd had so much in common. We shared a lot of the same dreams, goals, and aspirations. We both knew that we wanted to be successful in life. Mona had left and moved to Chicago; her mom's job had transferred her there. When Mona had graduated from high school, she'd returned to Cleveland to live with her dad. When we'd reconnected, it had been as if she had never left; we had not missed a beat. Mona had not finished cosmetology school in Chicago. She returned to the school where we met, and both ended and gotten our licenses together. We worked our first jobs together and had reached our first apartments at the same time but in different neighborhoods. We even bought our first new cars together, and they were candy-apple red. Man, we thought we were so fly.

One thing that I had always admired about Mona was her work ethic. Her work ethic was just like mine. We worked hard. Although we were very much alike, we were still very different. I was a girly girl and fashion stylist, and she was an emerging hip-hop rapper known as Mona D. Mona always put herself in a position to be around people who could help her get to the next level. She connected with people who made it possible for her to be a regular on the most popular radio stations in Cleveland. Although I had other friends, Mona was different. She was not hung up on any guy, and neither of us had kids. We were able to travel and make moves when we wanted to. With Mona, I was able just to live life, and it was fun and exciting. Not only did we dream, but we also made things happen. We were like Gayle and Oprah. Mona came from two very strong parents, and she had to take on a lot of responsibilities at an early age. She was definitely a daddy's girl, and she was tough. I was a spoiled brat, and it drove Mona crazy. Mona was not just my best friend, but it was like I had another sister.

We took abandoned salons and made them thrive. We were always booked months in advance, and if you were not getting your hair done by one, you were getting it done by the other. We complemented each other. Where I was weak, she was strong, and when she was weak, I was strong. We made a lot of salon owners rich and brought recognition to their salons because of our presence. When we left a salon, it was evident that our presence was no longer in the building.

Not only did we make a name for ourselves in Cleveland, but we began to make a name for ourselves outside of Cleveland. Mona was behind the scenes, working as a shampoo assistant for a national hair company.

I always said, "Mona, can you get me in? Because I want to work there too."

She always responded that they had no openings at the time. One day a sales rep came into the salon that we were working in, and I asked if there were any opportunities to become a platform artist. She said she would check into it and let me know. She came back to the salon two weeks later to inform me that one of the companies named Kizure was interested in interviewing me in Atlanta, Georgia. She asked me if I could get to Atlanta for the Bronner Brother's Hair Show. I asked if there was room for two because I didn't want to leave my friend Mona behind. I was always looking out for Mona, even when she was not looking out for me. We both were hired.

CHAPTER 18

The Salon

Since being back in Cleveland, I had so much on my plate and so many loose ends to tie up. I was running around like a chicken with its head cut off. I was doing everything while I was still without transportation. I needed to get a car. Next, I needed to find my own place to live. Living in a room at my sister's house with my two kids was becoming a bit overwhelming. Despite my situation every day, I was on my grind. I had to get Lauren situated and in her dorm at Kent State. I had purchased pretty much everything she needed while we were still in Atlanta. Allyson also had to get ready for school; she needed school uniforms and supplies. Those gift cards from Lauren's party sure came in handy. I needed to look for a house and a car with not much money.

Mona and I finally agreed on a location for The Salon. It was a mess. It had major potential if we could only get pass the Pepto Bismol-pink and the 1976-style wallpaper. Mona claimed she didn't have any money, although she was working two jobs and collecting unemployment. We decided and agreed on each of our responsibilities within the business. Mona was not a people person at all, so we decided that it would be best for her to handle the things behind the scenes, such as the contractors, electricians, paint, flooring, etc. Mona didn't have the cash; her contribution would be her unlimited Home Depot credit card. She would be able to purchase the things needed, using her card. She said she could utilize different people to do the work given, that she had already established good relationships with different people while working at "The Church."

I would be responsible for the operation of the salon. I would be the face of the salon, hire and train the stylists. I would be responsible for the working equipment, such as shampoo bowls, dryer chairs, pedicure and manicure stations, and also the products needed in the salon. I would set the standards for the salon and create the salon handbook. Together Mona and I came up with the operating procedures.

I ran an ad in Cleveland's local hair magazine, letting my clients know that I was back and in business. It wasn't two weeks before my phone was ringing off the hook. I began doing hair in an unfinished salon, and that is how I made the money I needed for my portion of my investment in the business. We became bigger than we were. The salon's name was ringing throughout the city. Mona was using the contacts she had in the radio industry for radio advertisements. We were marketing like we were a million-dollar salon, and we didn't even have floors or walls. We had a point to prove. I was on the comeback, and I was going to make it happen with my two daughters. Together we were going to show the Hermans we were back. Finally, The Salon was complete, and all of our hard work had paid off. By this time, I had put in eight thousand dollars cash to Mona's nine thousand dollars on her credit card. We had set this amazing salon together for under twenty thousand dollars. We realized we needed a few more things, but we were short approximately three thousand dollars.

I had no more money to give because I was in the process of moving into my house. What are we going to do? Mona and I decided to ask our mutual friend Nikki; she came through with no questions asked. She and Mona were already in business together, and I was working for them making three hundred dollars a week as a cook for their Kidz Catering Company when I first returned to Cleveland. Nikki was no joke. After she put in the money, she wanted to sit down and figure out how each person would get the investment that they had put into the business back. Nikki was adamant about getting a contract signed with all the particulars concerning this partnership, and so was I. Mona said that she would have our attorney put it together.

Mona asked, "Alaina, until we get on our feet, would you be willing to pay a commission to the salon?"

"What kind of commission?" I asked.

She said, "We need working capital, and I don't have any money."

All the while, Nikki was looking at me as if to say, "don't do it." This was our business, and I didn't want it to fail, so I did it anyway. I agreed for a period to pay 30% of the money I made to the business so that we would have working capital, and Mona paid nothing. Now it was time to fill The Salon, and because of our reputation in Cleveland within the hair industry, people wanted to work with us. We had a waiting list. We opened the salon with nine stylists, including myself. We were scared to death. We had no idea how this was going to work, but no one knew it. We began to turn Cleveland upside down, and we were making money hand over fist. We were able to get a space that was over two thousand square feet for eighteen hundred dollars a month with all utilities included. We were on top.

We fought about what was a fair commission fee for the stylists. Mona wanted it to be a 60/40 split with the stylists getting a 40% commission. Me being a stylist, I wanted things to be fair. This was one of the things I disliked about Mona. She was always on the bottom line. She said I didn't have business sense, and I said she was cutthroat.

We were able to move past it and come to an equal median of a sliding scale. We were now about six months into the business, and Mona was noticing that I was making money from working with clients on a regular basis.

She came to me and said, "Since you're making money, I need to get paid too."

I told her, "I make money because I do hair. You can make money too if you do hair. You're licensed just like me. You are not doing hair because you're choosing not to."

We had another meeting, and against my better judgment, we agreed to pay Mona $350 a week. The situation was getting very frustrating. The way Mona had set up to pay for things she needed to be done in The Salon was a bartering system. Contractors would do the work, and the stylists and myself were obligated to offer free services for spouses and children on a weekly basis until the debt was paid off. The stylists were beginning to get pissed off, and they began to complain. It was not only the fact that they felt they were being taken advantage of about the commissions, but also, they didn't understand why they were obligated to provide free services to clients and not be compensated for their work. I couldn't even help them or talk to them because I felt the same way.

The more money that came in, the more I began to see Mona change before my eyes. The Mona that I was afraid to go into business with had resurfaced. We still did not have a signed contract. Nikki and I asked Mona every other day about the contract, and every time she would have a different excuse. I was responsible for doing payroll as well as making the daily deposits. I was very aware of how much money was being made. We were making more than enough money for me to stop paying 30% commission into my own business. I felt that I should finally be able to work in my salon for free, but Mona was adamant about not doing that yet. She did not want that for me at all. Mona was the only one on the bank accounts, even though there were three of us involved with the business, with Nikki being the silent partner. My banking privileges had been destroyed from dealing with Al and his drug addiction. I was on every check system in the United States, so my not being on the bank accounts gave Mona power over me as a business partner. She said she didn't want Nikki on the bank account because in their other business she had terrible money management skills. She had bounced checks all over the place with the Kidz Catering Company. I was so confused because here she was in business with Nikki, and she was dogging her to me.

I needed answers, and Mona and I were no longer able to meet without arguing. Our relationship had become very volatile, so I set up a meeting with Nikki. I began to share my frustrations with her regarding all the money I put into the business and how Mona was getting paid, but I was getting nothing.

Nikki said, "I was looking at you when we had our first meeting like why you would agree to her terms? I asked Mona, I thought you said you all were best friends, so how could you do her like you are doing here? Nevertheless, I can fix this. Do you like Hummers?"

"Sure, I like Hummers," I said, wondering why she'd just asked me that.

"Would you like a Hummer?"

"Sure, I would like a Hummer, but how are you going to do that, because my credit is not good?"

"I have a Hummer, and Mona has a Hummer. Neither one of us pays for it out of our pockets. We don't pay for the car insurance or even our cell phone bill. I pay those items through our other business. Alaina, I open businesses for them to benefit me. It comes with perks, to own a business," she said.

"Well, it should."

"What color would you like?" Nikki asked.

"Black on black," I answered.

"Ok, I will call tomorrow and order everything you need, and it will be paid for by the business. All I need is for Mona to sign off on it because her name is the only one on the bank account."

Nikki explained how she had already run this by Mona, and she had not been at all in agreement. Nikki said that she'd asked Mona why this was such a problem.

Nikki told her, "You don't pay for yours, and Alaina is bringing in over fifteen hundred a week. She really could hold her note if she had to, but why should she? What is the problem?"

Now while Nikki was explaining this, all I could think about was how I had gone out my way to Mona. Every month when I received food stamps, I gave Mona a hundred and twenty-five dollars, so her family could have food in the house, even though she had a working husband. When I came back from Atlanta, I only brought back two sets of mattresses and our clothes. I gave Mona my twenty-five-hundred-dollar collection of Posturepedic double-pillow-top mattresses. She had cheap ones, and her husband was a big guy, and it was killing his back. I was living with my sister, and I was not using them. I helped take care of her daughter. When I got a few extra dollars, I would go and buy her clothes.

I waited, and a few days later, Nikki called me. She told me that the Hummer was ready to be picked up. All they were waiting on was Mona to sign off on it, and she refused. I was now trying to figure out what the hell was going on. She is worse than I ever thought.

Why would she not want me to have a car? I asked myself. She wasn't paying for it. Our business would be paying for it. Here it was: she wasn't as broke as she was claiming to be, and everything started falling in my lap, and I wasn't even looking for it. I was beginning to get suspicious, so I went to the bank and asked for a printout for the last six months, but they said they could only give me four months. Although I was not on the account, I was the one making all the daily bank transactions, so without looking, they assumed I was on the account and printed off the statements requested. I went home, sat down with a highlighter, and I went through those statements with a fine-toothed comb. I found out that not only was Mona getting her three hundred fifty dollars a week but I also noticed large payments were being made to her Home Depot account.

You have got to be kidding me, I thought. I was being played, used, manipulated, and pimped all at the same time. Mona was receiving fourteen hundred a month, and also receiving payments for her initial investment. Nikki and I were not receiving anything back on our investments.

Now my mind was going a hundred miles a minute. The receptionist and the stylists in the salon were acting funny toward me. I was trying to figure out what was going on. I have always tried to avoid the mess. One of the stylists named BeBe came to me and confronted me about something that I had supposedly said about her. I had no clue what the heck she was talking about. It was so far gone that it did not make any sense to me. I was always the type of person that if I said it, I owned it. I told BeBe we were going straight to the source. I called Mona and told her to get to The Salon as soon as possible because we had an emergency. She wanted to know what it was, but I would not tell her over the phone.

Mona came to The Salon, and BeBe and I were waiting to confront her. When she saw us, the first thing she said was, "Let's not talk inside. Let's go outside." Now I am not one for he said/she said, but BeBe was not playing. She told Mona everything that she had said that I was supposed to have said about her. Mona was nervous and denied having said anything. She tried to clean it up by saying that maybe BeBe misunderstood what she had said. This infuriated BeBe and me. I had seen Mona do this to other people for years, but I never thought in a million years that she would do this to me.

CHAPTER 19

True Colors

We're now almost two years in, and there was still no signed contract. Nikki and I were setting up meetings, and Mona had every excuse in the world as to why the contract was not ready. Nikki had put in three thousand dollars, but now I was in for over twenty-eight thousand dollars with the 30% commission that I had been sacrificing. I was there every day, running the salon as well as working in it, so I decided to take matters into my own hands since Mona didn't want to play fair. This was just as much my salon as it was hers, and I was the one doing payroll every week anyway.

I stopped paying the salon the 30%; instead, I often spent 10%, or sometimes nothing at all. I informed Nikki of what I was doing, and Nikki said I should have been doing that a long time ago.

Nikki said, "Alaina, there is no way I would be paying anything to my own business."

"Nikki, has she mentioned anything about our contract?" I asked.

Nikki laughed and said, "Girl, no. I must admit I am a little surprised that she is acting like this as well. When Herman fired her, and she was down, I gave her so much money to try to help her."

"Nikki, do you know I have been doing the attorney's hair for free for the last year and a half every two weeks for her services and still no contract.

"Alaina, why are you doing this?" Nikki asked.

"Nikki, I wanted the best for the salon, and I was willing to do whatever it took. Mona knew that I would, but it's about to stop."

"Good," Nikki replied.

She asked, "How are you and the girls?"

I said, "We're fine."

She asked, "How is Al?"

"It's funny you should ask 'cause he's doing well. He's back in Cleveland, and he has been clean for some months now."

"Do you think you all will ever get back together?" Nikki asked.

"We have been talking about it. I feel so guilty about divorcing him. I truly want my family back," I told her.

"Alaina, God can do anything. I'm going to pray for you both. What a testimony if your marriage is restored. Alaina, it is something about you and Al's relationship that's bigger than you and him."

"What do you mean?" I asked.

"I can't explain it, but when I saw you two last week at Allyson's game, God was all over you both. I don't believe he is done with you guys. Be very careful with who you talk to about you and Al because this is spiritual, and that's why the attack has been so strong against your family. Alaina watches Mona," Nikki stated.

"Thanks, Nikki. I appreciate that" I said.

It was so tense in the salon, but I didn't care because now I was dating my best friend again. We were taking it slow, but we were spending a lot of time together. He was there for all Allyson's basketball games and Lauren's performances. It was like old times. Mona figured out that we were getting back together, and she was pissed off. It made matters at the salon almost unbearable.

Mona was starting to show her true colors, so I began to spend less time there at the salon. I did hair Wednesday through Saturday. With Allyson's busy basketball schedule and my own life, the salon or stuff with Mona didn't faze me as much. Mona wanted to talk, so we did on a Monday while the salon was closed and I was doing payroll.

"Can we talk as friends?" Mona asked.

"Well, how else would we talk?" I asked her.

"Alaina, you know what I mean," she stated.

"No, really I don't. I have not changed at all."

Mona began to share her concerns about several things.

"Your presence is not here like it used to be. I mean, you are out of here on Saturday by noon. That is our busiest day. The stylist needs you, and you are nowhere to be found. When you leave, you don't even answer my calls. The stylist is saying things like, 'Momma Laine is never here anymore, and she is changing.'"

"Momma Laine" is what the stylist called me. They said I was such a mother. She went on to tell me how her daughter was missing me. Her daughter called me her angel.

She continued, "I am concerned about you. Are you getting back with Al? Alaina, please don't get back with him. You deserve so much better. You have been through so much."

I listened to what she had to say, but it was not what I needed to hear from her. Where is my contract? I thought. At this time, she did not know that I had a bank printout and that I knew she was taking money from the account. Nor was she aware that I had changed my pay scale. I was watching her mouth move, but I was not hearing anything she was saying. This woman right here was dangerous. She was not concerned about my kids or me. All while we were in Atlanta, she never did one thing for my children or me. She was making over six figures and never asked if we needed anything, and she knew what we were going through. I let her get everything she had to say out, and then it was my turn.

"Mona, you've known me since I was fifteen years old, and I have been very consistent. This is the reason I didn't want to go into business with you in the first place. We're so different in the way we handle business. I am concerned about you as well Mona. You have a five-year-old daughter that you don't spend any time with. She goes from one sitter to the next. She has poor manners and is extremely rude and disrespectful. You are so busy chasing a dollar that you forgot that you have a family. Your daughter needs you, and she needs consistency and boundaries. The reason she calls me her angel is because she knows I genuinely love her. Love is an action. You said that the stylists have been talking to you about some of their concerns. Well, they have been talking to me about their concerns as well. They hate it when you leave your daughter at the salon for hours, making them have to watch her even after her hair is done. They say she is a tyrant, and they don't want to be bothered. Just for the record, my children come first. They always have, and they always will. Allyson has basketball games every Saturday at one p.m., and I will never miss a game. I will never miss anything that my children participate in. This is not negotiable. You should try making your family a priority. I believe we should train one of the stylists here to be the manager. The responsibilities here are too much for me alone. We both own this salon, but I'm the only one doing anything. You're working two other jobs and getting paid from here. You have other sources of income coming in your house while I'm stuck here. I have other goals and dreams as well. I think BeBe would be a great manager."

She interrupted me and asked, "BeBe?"

I continued, "Yes, BeBe. This will relieve me of a lot of pressure and responsibilities so that I can do other things. I will continue to do the payroll and monthly meetings, but I will l only be a stylist and owner. You said I have changed, but I believe it is quite the opposite. This money has changed you. Let me show you something."

I got up, went to the back and grabbed a box of business cards that I'd found while I had been looking for something else. As I walked back in, she saw the box, and her eyes bucked.

She asked, "What's that?"

I said, "You tell me."

She was nervous as I opened the box, pulled out one of the cards, and slammed it on the counter. The card had the salon's logo and information on it. At the bottom, it read: Mona Dixon, Founder, and CEO.

"When in the hell did this happen."

She began to stutter and said, "I did not tell Jim to print that. He did it on his own. That doesn't mean anything to me."

She grabbed the whole box of cards and threw them in the garbage.

I asked, "What's going on? It was a different set up and logo."

As she tried to explain, I just shook my head.

I continued to answer the concerns that she had, and then I said, "You have one month to get the contract to me, or there are going to be problems. Neither the stylists nor I will do any more free hair to pay off anything else! I have put in over twenty-eight thousand into this business, and the BS stops now. Whatever the remaining balances are to the electrician, plumber, and our attorney, you will pay. You only put nine thousand into the business. As for my family and me, it is none of your business. What I decide to do with Al has absolutely nothing to do with you. This meeting is adjourned."

I left there feeling so empowered. Mona was probably like, What the hell just happened? She never expected me to respond like that. She was infuriated. The days ahead were going to be hell. Mona did not know what to do, so she began working her plan. She continued to turn the stylists against me, and because my presence was not in the salon as much, she had full rein. She made it so uncomfortable for me there. It was as if she was trying to get me irritated so I would quit. I continued to work, and she finally figured out what I had been doing with my pay. She tried to confront me, but I pulled out my papers showing how she was paying her Home Depot credit card. She began to tell the receptionist, the stylist, and the people in the city that I was stealing from our salon. I never said a word to defend myself, because while she was working her plan, I was working my plan with the help of Nikki.

Things had quieted down, but they were still very uncomfortable. Al and I had remarried and were back in ministry. Mona was openly pissed and telling people how stupid I was for getting back with him. I felt like I was cheating on Mona because I was back with Al. She was so controlling, her presence was felt when she would enter the salon, and it was evil and demonic. We got into a huge argument one day.

She said, "You don't have any idea what I am going through because I am in business with you."

"What are you talking about?" I asked.

"Just know that it has been hell for me."

I said, "Well, we can stop the hell now. Give me my investment back. I can walk away today and never look back!"

A few weeks passed, and I was still working. Bishop's wife was in the salon getting her hair done by me. I had her under the dryer. I walked to check to see if she was dry, but as I got close, I saw Mona sitting next to her, and they were in a deep conversation. Mona was holding up her dryer. They were so deep into their conversation that they never acknowledged my presence. Now, this was extremely strange because they were not friends at all. They only knew each other because of me. Mona didn't have any kind words about Bishop and his wife. She would say that their church was a cult when I was a member there. It was Mona who told Al about "The Church." She said that she had a dream, and in her dream, she saw Al standing with Pastor Herman, side by side and working together.

I asked myself, what are they talking about? They finally finished talking, and I brought her to my station to finish her hair. She was uncomfortably quiet.

"Is everything ok?" I asked.

She said, "Yes."

I finished her hair, and then I walked her to the door. As I walked back to my station, I saw Mona, and she could not look me in the face. I knew something was not right. The environment in the salon had become toxic. I got sick to my stomach when I would have to go in there. Al was quiet about it because we were working on our family. We were finally in counseling with Pastor McCurry, trying to move forward. I was trying to leave our past behind us, but he did not trust Mona at all. I took as much as I could from her. There was still no contract. I was over twenty-eight thousand dollars and some change two years later. I could not do this one more day.

I called Nikki. It was right after my birthday. Nikki and I met, and I explained what was going on and what had happened with Bishop's wife. Nikki was not surprised.

"So, what do you want to do?" she asked.

"Leave," I said.

"Where will you go? Do you want your own salon?"

I said, "Maybe."

"I will set up an emergency meeting, and I will also look for you a turnkey salon."

That's what happened. We met on December 27 at Bob Evan's Restaurant. Mona came to the meeting late. Nikki was there with contracts and exit plan strategies.

"How will Alaina and I recoup our investments?" Nikki asked.

Nikki said, "Mona will pay the down payment toward Alaina's new salon and fifteen hundred a month until the twenty-nine thousand was repaid."

The contract was ready to be signed. Mona was livid, but it was two against one. She wanted Nikki to be on her side, but the right was right. Nikki remained neutral and sided with what was right. The tension was so high and volatile to the point that you could tell a fight was brewing. Before I let that happened, I got up and said some strong words to Mona, and then I left.

I went home and prayed, and then I talked to Al. I decided to leave The Salon sooner than later.

It was New Year's Eve, and I was booked. Mona and the receptionist, whom I had known since I was a teenager, had begun to give my clients to other stylists, saying that I was overbooked. I continued to work. I waited until I was done with all eighteen clients. I packed up my personal belongings, which included my curlers, flat irons, stove, shears, and my blow dryer. I walked to the front where the night receptionist was counting the drawer, so I could take the deposit. There was one natural stylist left. It was pretty late at around 10:30 or so.

I said, "Thank you for all your help here at The Salon. This is my last day here."

"What? I knew something was not right. Mona's been calling here all night, asking to speak to different stylists. Does she know you're leaving?" she asked.

I explained that Mona knew, but she was not aware of the date. I refused to bring the new year in with this burden. I never said one negative word to any of the stylists. I didn't want to bring any more confusion to The

Salon. Mona and the receptionists had done enough. I walked away, while not taking anything I had purchased for The Salon and with almost twenty-nine thousand dollars on the table. It was one of the best decisions of my life. Nikki was also a real estate agent and had drawn up the deal. She came to the signing with a twenty-five hundred dollar check from Mona for the deposit. I could not believe it. The next month I received another check for fifteen hundred dollars, as agreed.

CHAPTER 20

Walking Away

A week later, I spoke with Bishop's wife, and I explained to her that I had left The Salon and walked away from my partnership with Mona. She was in disbelief. She wanted to know what happened. I began to explain to her the things that had been going on and how uncomfortable it was for me to be there.

She asked, "Do you remember that time when I was in The Salon underneath the dryer and Mona was talking to me?"

"Yes, I remember. I always wondered what you all were talking about because the conversation seemed so intense."

She said, "Mona came to me, and she was very nervous. She kept looking at me and saying, 'I don't know what to say or how to say it,' but the moment she opened her mouth I knew it was some mess. I felt like she was not sincere and upfront with me."

I said, "Well, what is it?"

"Mona, then says, 'I was in Herman's office for over two hours, and he along with some of his leaders were questioning and badgering me about why I'm in business with Alaina.' She said that since her husband is a member of the deacon board there, she should have never gone into business with you in the first place and where is her loyalty? Pastor Herman said that there were a bunch of rumors out in the street about him and Alaina. He said the rumors were put out there by my husband.

"I asked Mona if she was kidding me. I wondered what she was talking about because my husband doesn't even speak to Pastor Herman.

"Mona said, 'I know, and I'm so sorry that I am bringing this to you, but I am so uncomfortable. I didn't have anyone to talk to, and I didn't trust anyone else. When I saw you, I thought that I should share this information with you."

"Mona said she was in so much trouble for being in business with you that she didn't know what to do. I told her don't you ever repeat that again because my husband never said anything like that! I don't know where Pastor Herman is getting his information from, but that sounds nothing like what my husband would say."

I thought, is that all you said? You never said anything to try to defend me or my name in any way? That sounds just like your husband. Wow!

As the weeks went on, I finally opened my own salon, and I was able to continue working. My customers were starting to filter in slowly but surely. I found out from some of my clients that Mona was telling them that I had moved back to Atlanta, and I was no longer doing hair. She was also having the receptionist call some of my clients to suggest that they try other stylists in her salon and asking if they would like to book an appointment. It was pretty low down, but I thank God for my clients' loyalty.

My clientele took a hit out of this world. I went from making fifteen hundred dollars to two or three hundred dollars a week in a short period. I thought maybe it was because I had moved to the other side of town, or perhaps it was because I was so consumed with the fact that Al and I had remarried and were now the owners of our own salon that Nikki had put together for me. Maybe it was because I was back in the ministry. I just couldn't put my finger on it, but I later found out that supposedly I was being blackballed throughout the city by Pastor Herman. People were told that they could not do business with me or get their hair done by me. Now, this was much like the conversation Mona had shared with Bishop's wife.

They were even forbidden to have a conversation with me or my family. I was wondering, why in the world would this man be going after me to try to destroy my life after I have already gone through so much? Why would these people let him tell them who they could and could not talk to?

I had to stop giving this so much energy. It had started to consume me. I had so many other things going on. Our ministry was growing. We had opened a drug rehab center and a sober house. We had accomplished this in such a short time. After being in ministry for almost seven months, we started to outgrow our church and began to look for another place. We were doing very well. We found a new location, and we were to move in the next month, but that month came and went. Al relapsed again and took everything that I had worked for. The church, sober house, and the rehab center were empty. He had cleaned us out. I was bankrupt, emotionally, spiritually, and financially. To top it all off, Mona decided that she was stopping the monthly payments that she had agreed to. Not only did I walk away from the salon partnership with a loss of $25,000 on the table, but I also walked away from Al. It was for good this time. We were separated for a year, and then I filled divorced a year later. I had stood by Al through thirty-nine rehabs.

I'd never done anything to the Hermans or Mona. If I was guilty of anything, it was only of being faithful to my husband and my family. I never had an affair, smoked crack, or intentionally hurt God's people. I did not do anything, and still, I was treated this way. Even though Al did these things, he should have never been treated like he was being treated. It should never be the position of the church to throw God's people away no matter what the sin is. The Bible says in Galatians 6:1, "Brethren, if a man be overtaken in a fault, ye which are spiritual, restore such a one in the spirit of meekness; considering thyself, lest thou also be tempted."

This was still mindboggling to me. I thought, maybe all of this came from Mona. You can never track down a lie. All you can do is keep living your life. Now as I'm looking back, maybe Mona purposely did all of this. Perhaps she sold our thirty-plus years of friendship to get back in good graces with the Hermans. She could not get over being fired and not being connected to what was hot in the city. Once again, Mona had worked her hands to get herself back on top, and it had worked. Lady Herman and Mona could not stand each other, and now they were the best of friends. The church should never be a place that you seek to put yourself in the limelight. I'm not sure why, but I do know this: what's done in the dark will come to light.

You see, leadership can be a very dangerous position for pastors if you do not know how to handle the power that comes with it. Although they went to great depths to continue to try to keep me down, it did not work. I continued to push and thrive. I should have given up, and at some point, I did after all the hurt and pain I went through with leaders, pastors, and their wives here in Cleveland and Atlanta. I dealt with a drug-addicted husband and with just so many other different things that would have caused many people to be shaken and give up. Although I may have been swayed and even contemplated giving up, I never, ever gave up my faith in God, which is the only reason I'm writing this book. With tears in my eyes, and when I couldn't speak, I would utter the words, I trust You. I found out that the Holy Ghost did more than make you speak in tongues. It had keeping power because it kept me.

I put my trust, and my faith in the Jesus Christ who I knew would be able to bring me out of my turmoil. He kept me from having multiple nervous breakdowns. He kept my mind. He became my sustainer, my all-in-all, and my everything. My grandmother and my great aunt used to talk about who God was to them. Now I knew firsthand, and it had become a reality for my children and me. I don't know where we would be without Him. He did not just keep us; He protected us so much that my kids and I don't even resemble what we been through. I am forever grateful.

~~The Conclusion~~ - The Beginning

I want to thank God for choosing me to go through this. I know without a shadow of a doubt that God handpicked me. He believed in me. He knew that I would handle whatever the devil brought my way. He also knew that when He brought me out of it, I would not try to take any credit for any of this. Nor would I allow anyone else to take credit. I would give all accolades, all glory, and all honor to Him. I didn't always cross every T or dot every I. I made so many mistakes along this journey. The one thing I didn't do was quit. I had two goals on this journey. The first goal was not to disappoint God, and the second was not to disappoint my children.

Today I can honestly say that I am free from all bitterness and unforgiveness. It took me almost eleven years to get here. I now can say that I love the Hermans and everyone that they influenced to turn against me, especially Mona, because she went to great depths to build an army against me--people whom I helped raise and people who I had known since I was a child. I never fought back. I removed myself from everyone who was under her spell. The Bible says in 2 Chronicles 20:17 reads, "But you will not even need to fight this battle. Take your positions; then stand still and watch the Lord's victory. He is with you, O people of Judah and Jerusalem. Do not be afraid or discouraged."

I really feel bad for the Mona and the Herman's. They had huge things going on in the city, yet they continue to try to destroy me. I don't walk around calling myself a prophet, minister, pastor, or any of the titles that people in the church thrive on or get caught up on, although I have walked in all of them for over twenty-five years. The Bible is very clear in Psalm 105:15: "Touch not my anointed and do my prophet no harm."

I have also forgiven the Bishop and his wife. I don't know what they said or did not say. I handled this the way the Bible told me to in Matthew 5:23-24, New Living Translation (NLT): "So if you are presenting a sacrifice at the altar in the Temple and you suddenly remember that someone has something against you, leave your sacrifice there at the altar. Go and be reconciled to that person. Then come and offer your sacrifice to God."

And Mark 11:25 reads, "And when you stand praying, if you hold anything against anyone, forgive them, so that your Father in heaven may forgive you your sins."

I did not want anything to hinder my relationship with God, so I went and spoke to them separately at different times and explained how I felt about everything. There was nothing in this book about anything I said concerning our relationship that they were not aware of.

Not only have I forgiven them, but I have forgiven Al. I pray that God restores him. He is such a powerful man of God who got caught up. We made a promise to each other that we would never treat God's people the way we had been treated. I have not broken my promise. Anytime he needed me, and I could help, I would--from groceries to rides to work and church--and if he needed prayer, I was there. Al was not just my husband of twenty-four years; he was also my brother in Christ. I have never spoken negatively about him to our children. I have tried to help them remember the good things about their dad. I believe that Al still has work to do if he chooses to do so. Maybe now that I am free, he can become free so that we can help free others.

It was at that place in my life, at that time, when I was forced to make a choice. I could choose to give up, I could make excuses for myself, I could throw in the towel, or I could take the cards I had been dealt and play my hand.

Did the fairytale life I had planned work out? No, but that didn't mean that my life was over. It meant that God must have had another plan for my life. You see, we must be willing to let go of the life we have planned to have the life that is waiting for us.

I want each of you to remember this: failure is only permanent where resiliency fails to exist. Hardships should be expected. Life won't always go according to your plans. Like me, you may end up feeling as if you've failed at some of your goals. Even still, it is critical that you do not give up. You must keep going.

God made me a promise me when I stood on that stage over twelve and a half years ago. He said, Alaina, the same stage that man tried to bring you down on, the stage that you were humiliated on, the same stage that you were torn to pieces on for faults that were not your own, will be the same stage that I will restore you on, publicly.

Now I heard God say this, but it didn't seem like that was going to happen throughout this story. Instead of my situation getting better, it grew worse.

We persevered, even when it seemed like it would be easier just to withdraw. Today God is keeping his promise. He is putting me back on the stage and restoring my family, just like he said he would. I was resilient and trusted that He would keep his promise, and after twelve and a half years of depression, poverty, and isolation, I am beginning to see His true plan for my life.

Despite everything we've been through, my daughters and I are succeeding. My oldest daughter, Lauren, signed a record deal at sixteen and acted for Tyler Perry's House of Payne the same year, and she is finishing her last four classes for her bachelor's degree, with an upcoming music project set to be released.

My youngest daughter, Allyson, attends Howard University in Washington, DC. At the age of eighteen, she was the youngest elected official in the history of the nation's capital. She was invited by the First Lady of the United States, Michelle Obama, to speak at the White House, and she'll be heading off to England to study at the University of Oxford as a Luard Morse scholar. Allyson was also the 2016 Truman Scholar. She was featured in Essence, Ebony, and Glamour Magazine. They both served as BET's What's a State Ambassadors.

As for me, I am the founder and CEO of I AM Enterprises, a nonprofit organization that aims to empower our city's youth. We've worked with several hundred young people and equipped them with the tools they need to be successful. God said the principles that I gave you to raise Lauren and Allyson are the same principles I require you to give to other children.

If you are reading this book, you know that I am a published author, using my painful experiences in the church to help other people overcome. This is just the beginning. Romans 8:18 says, "For I reckon that the sufferings of this present time are not worthy to be compared with the glory that shall be revealed in us."

ALAINA HOLLOWAY-CARPENTER

Church Should be a Hospital

The church should be like a hospital. You don't expect to go to the hospital with a minor cold and leave with full-blown AIDS. You should expect to go and get directions and prescriptions to become healthy. Some sicknesses require stronger medicine and a longer recovery time according to the doctor's diagnosis. The doctors do not know everything. Sometimes they have to call in other physicians or specialists to figure out what is really going on. Some might be more familiar with the issue if it was their choice of study while in school, they have had similar symptoms, or know someone whom they have treated with this sickness before. The goal of the doctor is to give a remedy to the issue. Some sicknesses require long-term help while others can be in and out. Some can require surgeries and rehabilitation centers. Doctors do everything in their power to make sure that the patient understands what is going on as well as the path they need to take to get better. There are those times where the doctor cannot do anything to make the patient better, but that is only resolved after extensive testing and research. It is at that time that the doctor's staff tries to make the patient comfortable. The patient also has a responsibility to their outcome. They must follow the instructions of the physician. Take medications as directed and go to follow up appointments, therapy, and routine visits. This is to make sure everything is going well, and if it is not or if other problems occur, the patient can notify the physician at any given time so that something else can be done. The physician works with a skilled team that has gone through the proper schooling and training to be qualified to make such diagnoses. Everyone that is a part of the team has had different training from the medical receptionist, STNA, LPN, RN, the doctor, etc. They all have one goal as a team, and that is to ensure that each patient is restored to a healthy state. The staff or the team that is working with the patient is not always one hundred percent right and at times give the wrong medications or the wrong diagnoses that can be detrimental to the patient. It is at that time where the person who has misdiagnosed is dealt with. Depending on how severe the situation is will determine what measures of discipline that will be taken. It can be a fine, suspension up to a year, or license being taken away and never can practice medicine again. Physicians are held accountable for their actions by a board. These mishaps can leave patients severely worse off than they were when they came in, some even unto death. That is why it is extremely important to have someone who is qualified and verified who you trust to administer healing to you or family members. Your very life depends on it. You do not expect the doctor to be worse off than you and not take the information or directions on themselves first. They have the propensity to get sick or even be on meds themselves however you don't expect them to come in your room with an oxygen mask on, I.V.'s in their arms, runny nose, coughing all over you, bleeding and open wounds saying how I can help you? This is not to suggest that the doctor can't get sick or have life-threatening situations like anyone else. However, the physicians should at least be out of ICU before working on someone else. Some great doctors administer healing to patients every day, without them some people would not survive or have the ability to function in their basic everyday lives such as walking, taking, eyesight or life without pain. We are grateful for the medical institution and the employees that carry out the charge of saving lives every day however we do not make them gods. We take the information or even the testimonies of our own experience to show someone we know or who runs across our paths that may be suffering from the same things you were just experiencing and refer them to who helped you in hopes that it can be a help to them as well. In church, sometimes the pastors and the leaders of the church are just as sick as the members. They have suffered sexual abuse, lack, low self-esteem, emotional neglect, depression, mental illness and the list could go on, and they never receive the proper attention to reach a place of healing in their personal lives. They learn how to cover up and continue this journey of faith without ever addressing the issues that they suffer. The saying "Hurt people hurt people" is very true. In this saying, I don't believe that the hurt is intentional, but what's in you is bound to come out knowingly an unknowingly even at the expense of others. In my opinion, a lot of Christians hide behind the pulpit or the aspect of religion or doing church work thinking that is the cure-all for being healed from their past hurts which was never dealt with. It's in this place where we learned how to be fake, phony and judgmental never dealing with our demons from childhood pain. It is a trick of the enemy to keep us bound and never to experience the abundant free life that God has intended for the believer. Doctors have accountability but not often do pastors have that, which is why the cycle continues. Some pastors lie, steal, cheat, rape, take advantage of members and so much more yet they continue to get in the pulpit Sunday after Sunday never dealing with anything and continues to inflict pain on a daily basis. People get mad and leave churches regularly, and they are never healed. They take their pain with them and move to another church to another pastor who left because he was hurt, and he never dealt with his pain. The cycle continues, and Jesus Christ dying seems to almost be in vain because this was one of the reasons why He died. Churches are popping up every day on corners, in schools, movie theaters, hotels, community centers and living rooms. With wounded leaders who got mad and left and said that God called them to pastor. Now you have wounded and broken leaders trying to pastor wounded and broken members. Unlike doctors who must go to school for at least eight to twelve years minimum pass medical examination and complete one year of medical residency to ensure the student knows what they are doing. In this field and so many other professions you cannot become licensed if you have certain things on your record. Not for a Pastor all you need is to say that you had a dream and God called you to pastor, put on your black suit and white clergy collar and pay your fee to be acknowledged by the state. No education, background checks or anything. Pastors continue to break every commandment one through ten, spend church money after receiving their lofty salaries and all the perks that comes with it...houses, cars all in the churches name, molest children, sleep with members in the church and have every member of their family on the church's payroll whether they are qualified for the position or not and scattering the sheep that God supposedly called them to shepherd... Who holds the pastor accountable?

Ezekiel 34:1-12

1 The word of the LORD came to me:

2 "Son of man, prophesy against the shepherds of Israel; prophesy and say to them: 'This is what the Sovereign LORD says: Woe to the shepherds of Israel who only take care of themselves! Should not shepherds take care of the flock?

3 You eat the curds, clothe yourselves with the wool and slaughter the choice animals, but you do not take care of the flock

4 You have not strengthened the weak or healed the sick or bound up the injured. You have not brought back the strays or searched for the lost. You have ruled them harshly and brutally.

5 So they were scattered because there was no shepherd, and when they were scattered, they became food for all the wild animals.

6 My sheep wandered over all the mountains and on every high hill. They were scattered over the whole earth, and no one searched or looked for them.

7 Therefore, you shepherds, hear the word of the LORD:

8 As surely as I live, declares the Sovereign LORD, because my flock lacks a shepherd and so has been plundered and has become food for all the wild animals, and because my shepherds did not search for my flock but cared for themselves rather than for my flock,

9 Therefore, O shepherds, hear the word of the LORD:

10 This is what the Sovereign LORD says: I am against the shepherds

and will hold them accountable for my flock. I will remove them from tending the flock so that the shepherds can no longer feed themselves. I will rescue my flock from their mouths, and it will no longer be food for them.

11 For this is what the Sovereign LORD says: I myself will search for my sheep and look after them.

12 As a shepherd looks after his scattered flock when he is with them, so will I look after my sheep. I will rescue them from all the places where they were scattered on a day of clouds and darkness.

Churches are no longer safe havens, and the word of God is no longer the standard. Churches have become big business, and God is not pleased...Judgment is coming! Not just for the leaders and their wives but for those who have sat in leadership and have closed your eyes to this foolishness you are just as much at fault. Judgment is coming to you too...

The Altar Call

Maybe you have read this book, and you can identify with one or more of the characters. Maybe you are a bishop, a pastor, a first lady, a PK (pastor kid), or an armor-bearer, and you have found yourself abusing the power that came with the position or abusing the people whom God called you to lead. We have all sinned and fallen short of the glory of God. Perhaps you are on the praise team, finance committee, or parking ministry, or you are a choir member, musician, altar worker, deacon, or usher. Maybe you are not the abuser, but you have been abused. Wherever you may find yourself, God is here right now to forgive and to set you free. This is the only altar where the abused and the abuser can come at the same time and be forgiven by the same God! I had to come to the altar first to ask God to forgive me. He is so loving, so forgiving, so kind, so patient, and so long-suffering. There is absolutely nothing we could ever do to deserve his love and forgiveness, but it's free to the believer. God is faithful and just to forgive us of our sins. Don't allow pride, bitterness, and unforgiveness to keep you from experiencing the abundant life that God has for you!

Maybe you are reading this book, and you have never accepted Jesus Christ as your personal Savior. Today can be the first day of the best days of your life. Say this prayer: "Dear Lord Jesus, I know I am a sinner, and I ask for your forgiveness. I believe you died for my sins and rose from the dead. I trust and follow you as my Lord and Savior. Guide my life and help me to do your will. In your name, amen."

If you prayed this prayer, congratulations for making the best decision of your life!

www.ingramcontent.com/pod-product-compliance
Lightning Source LLC
Chambersburg PA
CBHW070426010526
44118CB00014B/1913